Our Living Mind
Being Alive (Book One)

Lewis Holt

Copyright © 2022 Lewis M. Holt

All rights reserved. No part of this book may be reproduced or transmitted in any form or by any means, electronic or mechanical, including photocopying, recording or by any information storage and retrieval system without permission in writing from the publisher.

Blue Rose Books—Carbot, AR
Paperback ISBN: 979-8-9874412-0-6
eBook ISBN: 979-8-9874412-1-3
Library of Congress Control Number: 2022923496
Title: *Our Living Mind | Being Alive (Book One)*
Author: Lewis Holt
Digital distribution | 2022
Paperback | 2022

Dedication

Dedicated to all of those who tend to approach their Life as an opportunity for improving themselves.

Contents

Preface vii
Introduction.. xi
Part One 1
Part Two.. 25
Part Three.. 47
Part Four 67
Part Five.. 89
Afterword 112

And So...

Love is my Shield...
Joy is my Spear...
Truth is my Refuge...
... and Never really Claiming Myself (as such)
is my Reality...

And I have a little story here that has been passed down through *Zen* tradition these many centuries, that I suppose we could just call: a slight *Preface* of sorts...

There was once a very wise old man who long ago lived in China. Seeking a quite Life, he lived out in the country, well away from others. He had a delightful little dwelling, at the base of a large and pointed hill; of the kind that we so often see in pictures of China. Coming home late one night from a visit to friends, he surprised a thief in his house.

Now the old man well knew that there was nothing of any real value in his house that the thief could have possibly wanted. So looking somewhat embarrassed, the old man began to take his clothes off, folding them and laying them neatly upon a bench that was there, just inside of his doorway. "I am so sorry," the old man was saying to the thief, "that you have come all of this way... but that there was nothing here in the house of any value."

He picked up the neatly folded clothes from the bench, and walking over to the thief offered him the clothes. "Here… these are my best clothes, and might be worth a *little* something. Please, accept them as a gift… so that you will not have to go away empty handed." The thief looked at the old man like he was looking at a crazy person. But nonetheless, he grabbed the clothes from the old man's hand, and ran out of the house and down the road.

The old man stood in the doorway for a while, and he watched until the thief had disappeared into the shadows of the darkened road. Then he slowly moved over to a wooden stool which he kept in front of a large open window, and he sat down. Sitting there naked, he gazed out of the window at the full moon; which hung in the sky just above the tree line. How large and full and rich it looked.

And how sweet and fresh the night air smelled… while the sounds coming from out of the darkness, were like an enchanting melody, being played in a virtuoso clutter, of togetherness and discord, by all of the tiny creatures surrounding the old man's house. The shadows from the moonlight, both inside of the house, and outside upon the grounds, were haunting and seductive: almost alive.

A very mild and gentle breeze was blowing through the doorway —that the thief had left open in the haste of his flight; and which the old man hadn't bothered to close. Such beauty. It was as though the old man lived within the very gardens of paradise. Or at least that's how the old man saw it. But then as I say, he was very old, and very wise.

He sat there in perfect contentment and peace. After a while he looked towards the road in the direction that the thief had taken, and he sighed. "Poor fellow…" he mused, thinking of how forsaken the thief's eyes had seemed… the eyes of a man with a steady diet of hopelessness, and despair. "I wish I could have given him this beautiful moment."

He sighed again.

Introduction

Once you read this introduction, and then read the narrative that follows, you might well wonder why we actually called this little segment an "introduction." Because it doesn't really: "introduce" *the subject matter* of the narrative.

But then, you couldn't really say that it is wholly without purpose. Because what is perhaps even more important than introducing the subject matter of the text... what this section actually *does* introduce, is well let's say: "the frame of mind" that prompts an investigation, into the kinds of topics that we will be exploring here.

(So... if *that* serves at all...).

1. "... to be alive..."

If I were going to write the coolest poem ever, I think that would be it right there; just those three words: "to be alive." I mean it would be pretty hard to get more to the point of things than that. Yet sadly, we tend to take being alive pretty much for granted; as though just the event itself was really no big deal —as though "being alive" was just something that we needed to be, in order to drive our automobile around, and to go to parties and such.

But when taken by itself, and examined as strictly *a phenomenon*, the condition of being alive is really quite the amazing circumstance; isn't it? Just totally unique, and absolutely without parallel.

But yet like I say, every one of us is thoroughly guilty, of disregarding the utter *awesomeness*, and *the wonder* of just: being alive; and instead (as I say: are thoroughly guilty) of looking at our Life as merely a "tool"… something *to use* for pursuing "the important things in Life" (you know: acquiring wealth and prestige; and getting people to like us; and things of that nature).

But the whole while, without our really seeming to even notice it, being alive is laying some utterly fabulous riches right at our very feet. It is bestowing us, just by its very nature, with *gifts* of such rare magnitude, as to make a bucket of pearls seem like, well… just so much sand.

And my whole point is, we're really missing the boat, you know? I mean, we pine over our lack of creature comforts; or an overcooked roast; or even a pimple. While we allow the most extraordinary phenomenon that anyone *could ever imagine*, to pretty much just slip through our fingers.

Now I really don't want this to sound like, you know one of those: "we should stop and smell the roses" sort of things —as uplifting as those themes may at times be.

But I *would* like to touch upon a few things, that we perhaps don't really tend to think about very much; but which nonetheless, are worthy of a little examination. And in the process, let's see if we can't "build a case" as it were, for being alive (as flippant and gratuitous as that may sound). And you know, see how it actually "stacks up." See if it's really worthy of, well let's say: its reputation among poets.

2. And to that end, the first thing that I think we should do is to take a quick look at some of "being alive's" competitors —some of its competition for our entertainment dollar.

Oh wait a minute though. Hmm... Actually there *is no* competition is there? Because apparently, as it turns out, "being alive" is the *sole source* of experience. Experience of any kind, anywhere. I mean, wouldn't you think so?... So that's got to be something that we can put over in the "plus" column. But let's see what else we can dig up.

Well... being alive endows us with some really amazing natural abilities. Qualities which took nature literally *eons* to develop and perfect; and which are nothing less really, than just some utterly cool stuff. Take for instance our physical perception —which, and may I say, *unbelievably*, we all tend to completely undervalue as a thing in and of itself... (as we rush along, all caught-up in the business of our daily lives).

Now by way of illustration, let's suppose that you are under some sort of severe strain at work. The project that you and your team have been working on is beginning to lose its momentum; and every day, its expected completion date is becoming more and more of a forlorn hope. Further, everyone on your team has been —rather unrealistically— depending *upon you*, for some sort of tour de force; to break the whole thing out of its developing complacency.

And to top it all off, your supervisor has caught wind somehow of the project's floundering; and has taken it upon himself, just this very morning, to exhibit great ingenuity and creativity, in "chewing you a new one."

So to put it mildly, you're sunk way down in the doldrums of despair; with no intimation of even a slight breeze that could start filling your sails, and begin moving you out of such a predicament.

3.   But just stop and take a moment to look at what *your eyes* are doing. Look at all of the strange colors, and unusual shapes, and bizarre textures that they're perceiving. And look at the depths of field that you're able to distinguish, with no trouble at all. And with just a slight glance in either direction, you're suddenly aware of everything that's going on all around you: cars you have to avoid; things you need to keep from bumping into; menacing looking people; etc. etc.

I invite you reader if you would, to join me in a little experiment designed to "showcase" the marvelous effect of "*seeing*." And what we're going to need to do: is to "turn off our mind" and just, *use our eyes*. *Experience* them… *consume* what they are doing.

We can do this sitting down; or if it's not too inconvenient, we might even "get up" and *slowly* walk around the room. And *USE* the eyes; manipulate their focusing. That is…

… while moving your eyes freely around the room —and with a "light (and 'relaxed') touch"— *play* with their "focusing." Bring both eyes into focus on objects close to you; then focus on objects a little farther away; and then bring objects even further away than that into focus…

… and then, shift around between these distances. In other words (in as enjoyable a manner as possible) keep changing "the focal point" of your eyes as you move them around the room; and remember: "go lightly"…

... then, focus on shapes; and focus on colors. Focus on *the contrast* of shapes; and the contrast of colors... and the contrast *between* shapes and colors...

... pay attention to the depths of field you perceive between objects, and how these depths of field give dimension and perspective to the world around you...

... and the whole time that you are manipulating the focusing of your eyes, and manipulating how "they dwell" upon the different aspects of perception, apply yourself to creating: *entertaining and unique* images, and "interesting compositions" and things like that...

... (and while you go about doing all of these things, periodically stop and close your eyes... so that you can keep demonstrating to yourself, what this would all be to you, if *you couldn't see*)...

... and so on, and so on... etc. etc. etc. Just do everything that your eyes *will do*.

Okay. Ready? *GO!*

Da, da, da, da... humn, humn, humn...

... Are we back? ... *Alright!* Now tell me; could you *even imagine* something more unique and delightful than seeing!?!...

And if you're really not *duly impressed*... trust me: *you're not doing the exercise correctly*. Because you can put together some really *stunning* perceptions, by manipulating what your eyes do!

(And actually, once you get the hang of this, you could even "treat yourself" all day long on these kinds of "little tidbits."

(And I suppose I might mention, since we're right here anyway... that performing a routine similar to our little experiment here [or really, just some little *portion* of such a routine]... two or three times a day or so —or just whenever you feel like it— is in fact *great exercise* for the eyes; and will help to make the eyes more "mobile," and "effective."

(Indeed, these sort of "exercises" will actually help *to improve your vision.* Because poor visual acuity is almost *never* a result of "bad eyes"; but instead is almost *always* a result, of "the state of mind" behind *the use* of the eyes. Which is to say that basically, it is a product of: *HOW* you use your eyes.

(So: relax, and don't strain; and slowly "*build up*" the keenness of your vision [like you would build up the strength of your arms]).

4. Or how about appreciating what your ears do: hearing? What a tasty *depth* they give to the world around us. Are you listening? (Pun intended). Are you *perceiving* this depth? (If you're in your house, "*reach into*" another room for a moment or two with your hearing. And then for comparison, "pull yourself back," and plug your ears with your fingers. *Now* try to "reach." You can't do it. You can't "feel" this "depth" without your hearing. Is that strange or what?)

And the really unique thing about hearing, is that it extends the depth that it gives to the world, *well beyond* our immediate field of attention. Which besides being at times really functional, is just a totally cool phenomenon: hearing a dog barking far in the distance; or a train go by some blocks away; or a radio playing through someone's window.

And how about the crown jewel of hearing? Hearing enables us to *freely communicate* with our fellow beings —by *hearing* what they're saying to us. And thusly of course, we are then able to completely grasp (at least ostensibly) what it is that they are trying to express. Now how cool *is that*? (H. C. I. T.)?

And while we're right here talking about our physical senses, how remarkable and bizarre of an experience is our ability *to feel* things; or to smell; or to taste food? Feeling the hardness of wood, or the softness of skin, or the roughness of fabric; the smell of burning leaves in the distance, or of freshly cut grass... the smell of a baby; the taste of bacon (or how about eggnog?)...

Okay! So I think that we can definitely consider physical perception, *to absolutely* be one of our Life's chief endowments. But how about some of the other natural abilities that we possess? Like for instance: "the pure joy" let's call it, of physical movement. Our body —which conveniently enough, is gathered into a nice and neatly contained package— can stand up and move itself from here, to over there. Or it can bend over to tie its shoe laces; or climb a tree to score some cherries; or raise a bottle of brewski to our lips.

And we might mention that this quality of physical movement is actually, *not shared* by all living beings. There are plenty of Life-forms out there, who *don't even possess* arms and legs (nor lips either for that matter). But as I say, for things which bring enjoyment to our existence… it's hard to beat the sheer simplicity of movement.

5.   But our Life doesn't just take place, solely within the realm of *our physical* attributes. If we're looking for things that add dimension and diversion to our existence, how about considering the qualities of our active intelligence —traits like: being curious, and wondering about things (what's over there on the next counter; or: why does water really freeze)?

I mean, the act of: *"wondering"* is really *an enjoyable* experience. It's so diverting, that you can even just sit there in a "daydreaming-like trance," *and do nothing, but* "wonder." And yet you would be thoroughly entertained. (You don't even really need to be wondering *about* anything in particular; but just sort of "basking in the energy" of wondering. Try it out…).

Or how about our ability to conceive: of "ourself" —you know, to be able to visualize the idea of "me"? (A computer has no such idea; but *our* existence would be pretty bland without it). Or how about: thinking? Now is that a strange and unique ability, or what? Or perceiving the passage of time —just relaxing, and watching a moment move lazily along…? I mean these are *exquisite* events: every one of them! *Aren't they*?

And of course we can't forget "the feelings," of emotions and passions. Things like: love and joy, and hope, and happiness; and even things like: sadness, and envy; despair, even…

(Though we tend to distinguish between so-called: "positive, and negative" emotions, and passions; just the same, *both* have the potential to be extremely rich and full experiences. I mean, either can be: enthralling and all-consuming. Like: *rage*. Don't you think that a person in a rage, is "*enjoying* himself silly"? He's just *totally engrossed* in what he's doing, you see. He's *completely "diverted."* [Though these types of radical behavior in the end, are *extremely taxing* upon our constitution])!

… the joy of loving your child; or the rapture of your mate's embrace; or the simple happiness of lolling in your backyard in a reclining lawn chair, on a beautiful spring day… your eyes closed, while you bask in the warmth of the sun... a gentle breeze bringing you the fragrant aromas of freshly cut grass, and "sweet flowers" (umm, honeysuckle...). Oh yeah!

Or if you want to get to the real brass tacks of experience, how about the act of simply being "conscious" (you know: "being awake")? Now there's *a real* show-stopper. In fact you'd be pretty hard put to think of something, well let's say, more *consuming* than being conscious.

6. What I'm trying to say here is that, it's hard to see how anyone could fail to enjoy themselves blue; when we've got all of these really great experiences —this array "of magnificent toys" (as it were)— basically, just: at our very beck and call.

Indeed, when we consider the great bounty of priceless treasures allotted us by Life... the grandeur of it is so utterly overwhelming, that it's really as if we actually existed *in paradise itself* —as the old man in our *preface* imagined.

And the curious thing here is, that's exactly what "holy men" of every ilk and measure, have been *trying to tell us* for centuries. They say that, *it is indeed* as though we existed in paradise itself; but yet somehow, were *unaware* of the uniqueness of our position; were unaware of our extraordinarily good fortune.

You see, these holy men say, we allow "the burden" of being alive... to *so monopolize* our thoughts, that we leave ourselves *little time*, to focus upon Life's splendor.

And don't get me wrong here. I'm not looking at Life through rose-colored glasses; by any means. I'm as well aware of "the hell" of being alive as the next person is. I mean, I can see physical pain; and I can see unfulfilled longing. And I can see missing limbs; and debilitating diseases…

… and delayed flights; and flat tires; and the fatigue of old age; and… your computer screen suddenly going blank! And whatnot, and what have you.

("… whaddaya *mean* you're all outta chocolate milk!!?!").

But even in the face of this onslaught, from what I suppose we might call: the harshness of reality; I just don't see how —if we were to turn and "face the other direction" as it were; and take a moment for pause and consideration— how we could fail to establish, well let us say, a more "manageable perspective" of the current circumstances… by recognizing, and appreciating: the utter *awesomeness* really; the true *wonder*; and indeed, the unfathomable *mystery*… of just… being alive.

Our Living Mind

Part One

Chapter 1

1 If you can read this page, and do other things like: watch television, and ride a bicycle, and oh I don't know... eat a sandwich (although not all necessarily at the same time), I'd say it's a pretty fair bet that you're probably alive.

("... uh... o-kaay...").

But do we ever stop to ask ourselves what that really means: "to be alive"? What I'm saying is, what is it about us that actually *makes us* alive; that makes us a living being?

Is it our body really? Are we alive merely because we have a working organism (that not only pumps blood, and secretes hormones, and things like that, but also) that can do things like walk, and talk; and see, and hear; etc. etc.?

Are these the things that make us alive then: our body's mechanical functions? I mean, are we alive just *because* we walk and talk, and see and hear?

What I'm saying is, is that what *creates* being alive for us: doing those things? Are we just a body that can go around doing things; and that's all there is to us?

2. Well no. There's more to being alive than just that, isn't there? We're not just some empty machine with no "soul" (with no *person* at the helm)... just some "robot" going around performing functions.

By no means. There is more depth to us than that.

We have a mind. I mean, we can think, and feel, and imagine. But you see, that's what we're trying to get to the root of here. What is it that actually *creates*... a state "of mind" within us? A state, of "being alive... *AS*... a living mind"?

(Because fundamentally, having a mind that can think, and feel, and imagine... well that's what being alive really is, isn't it)?

But if we're going to try to answer this question (of what actually creates *a mind* within our person...) perhaps we should see if we can't *define* this concept of "mind" a little better.

3. So first of all, instead of saying simply that: "we have a mind," let us instead say that what it is we all undeniably possess, is the quality... of "*sentience*." Alright. And what being sentient really means essentially is that: *we realize* that "we are alive."

So. And as what we might then call the "operational conditions" of being sentient, we (could go on to say that, *as sentient beings*, we) are each of us: actively "awake" (somehow). Our mind is conscious. (Which in effect is to basically say, that we are responsive to our environment).

And not only are we conscious, but we are also actively *aware*. I mean, we are perceptive of our circumstances; we know what's happening to us. (As constituents of an interactive environment, we can discern [and then fully recognize]... the scope of any situation, that our environment may confront us with).

So in other words, we're not just "awake to the world." We also *know* —that for instance (if you would)— we are sitting in this chair.

4. Okay. So we are a living organism that can do things —like see and hear; and walk and talk; etc. And not only this but, *as* an organism, we also possess a living mind; which is to say that we are awake and perceptive.

And of course beyond this (*because* we possess a mind [that is, because we are awake and perceptive]) we also realize that we are alive.

But here's the relevant question for us: as our body goes around seeing and hearing and everything... is this what actually *makes us* awake and perceptive? In other words what I'm saying is, is being conscious and aware merely "a product" of such abilities as seeing and hearing?

Are we conscious and aware *only because* of what our eyes and our ears, etc. do?

5. Do you see what we're after here? What we want to know is... is our organism (and its physical abilities) really "the sole, and singularly essential commodity" in being alive?

Or is there more to us than just our body and the things that our body does? Is there indeed something actually: "within the body (some 'essential quality,' or some 'inner nature,' or what have you)" —that isn't exactly the body itself; but nonetheless, is the part of us that actually makes the body alive... that makes it conscious and aware; that turns this "robot" into a living being?

I mean is the organism itself actually "our person"? Or is there some other quality involved?

Chapter 2

1 "*Seers*"... (those who are evolved in their knowledge of "the mysteries of Life": sages, prophets, mystics) say that what actually makes our person alive... is (not really our body, and the things that our body does; but is instead) an innate "*presence*" that resides within us.

Now of course, this may well just sound like a fancy way of not really saying anything at all —just a way of pretending that something is actually there, simply by giving it a name. ("... wow, like! You know... we're just some kind of... of 'presence.' *You know*?").

However, this "living presence" (as seers more fully refer to it) is really more than just some abstract concept. It is an actual energy. In fact, seers say that it is a small ball of intense white light (just beyond our range of perception)... that is sort of "hovering there": where our head joins to our torso.

the living-presence

Illustration 1

2. Now, when seers say that it is this ball of living presence which actually makes us alive, what they really mean is that, this energy is the part of us that actually *IS*... really alive. In other words, seers say that this ball of energy is in fact: *our real form of existence*.

What I mean is that, our organism isn't really our living being at all. Or to put this another way, the organism *is not* really the part of us that's awake and perceptive. It is not our real "person."

Instead, it is this energyball of living presence "within the organism," that is actually responsible for our person's awareness of himself, and for his responsiveness to the world around us.

3. So we can say that, this living presence is what really makes our organism "a living being." Because without this "presence," the organism is really nothing more than just… an operational mechanism; a big, hulking, biological *machine*.

It's just a mechanical system, fueled by organized chemical processes. I mean, it's not a living thing at all really. It's just… an apparatus.

Or to put this another way, we could say that the organism is just a "working system," that's not really capable of self-manipulation; but that in fact requires an operator (or a "driver") to be at all functional.

And this ball of white light that is "hovering" there, just beneath our head… *is* the organism's operator.

4. In fact, this ball of light is actually an "*energy Life form*"… who is alive, in and of itself (meaning that it is alive: exclusive of the organism).

Indeed, you could really say that, this energy Life form is essentially *inhabiting* the organism. The organism is just "a vehicle," for providing it with the means of interacting with the physical universe.

Seers are wont to call this energy of living presence our "enduring Life-form". Or sometimes they refer to it, as our "recurring Life-form." They say that it is the part of us that has "come to this world"; and the part of us that will someday "leave this world."

It is that within us which is customarily referred to as: our "spirit."

5. Actually though, it is not totally accurate to say that what this living presence inhabits is the organism itself. Instead what our spirit really inhabits, is an "energy system" which exists… in correlation with —or let's say, *coupled to*— the physical body; that seers call: "*the energy body*."

But we should really be more precise here. Because this system you see, is not normally dubbed: "the energy body"... *until*... it becomes inhabited by the living presence. Up until that time —or, when it is referred to independently of the living presence— it is usually just called: "*the luminous body*" (because well... its energy is "luminous."

([And what seers mean by calling this energy luminous is that, it emits light, but (as we shall see) is not exactly the source of that light]).

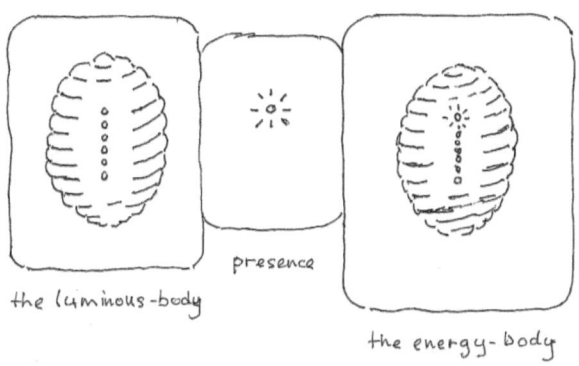

Illustration 2

6. From a practical point of view what this luminous body really is, is just an *energy machine* that is "connected" to the organism's brain, and other vital centers of operation; and is used for *controlling* the organism —for "driving it around," and getting it to do what our living presence wants it to do.

Now if this all sounds rather suspiciously to you as what "our mind" is supposed to be doing... well give yourself a gold star for paying attention.

Because in fact this "luminous body" —or more correctly it is rather *the union* you see, *between* the luminous body and living presence (which as I say we then call: the energy body)— is indeed just that very phenomenon which we commonly refer to, as *our mind*.

Chapter 3

1 But before we plunge into our exploration of all of this, we should probably mention that (as you have no doubt already discovered) the "luminous body" —like our living presence— is not exactly visible to the naked eye.

The reason for this (as we shall be seeing) is simply because, the living presence and the luminous body do not actually exist within, *this particular* "dimension of expression." Instead they really exist within (what seers call), a "dimensional *variant*" of this world.

Seers however, who have known about the energy body for millennia, have learned to use abilities of perception which exist within the mind itself —and which they simply call: the "mind's eye"— that allows them to directly perceive these living energies.

What I mean is that, seers are able to actually *see* the luminous body and it's living presence, as clearly as they are able to see the organism. (And anyone really can learn to do this).

But to return...

2. Now of course the most common conception of "the mind," is that it is some vague form of reference, to *our brain's* intellectual capacities —just a *term*, for referring to our thinking processes and such.

But contrary to this notion, the mind is in fact "a thing, in and of itself."

As I'm saying, it is a literal, field of energy (that has very definite form and substance); which exists quite independently of the organism (and the brain); though it is of course inextricably linked to the organism.

Indeed (and even though we have already applied this phrase to our living presence; nevertheless... as our luminous body is in essence, actually the "mortal extension" of our living presence... and the union *between* the luminous body and living presence is what actually *constitutes*: "our mind")... you might well say that *the mind itself* is really, "an energy Life-form, inhabiting our physical body."

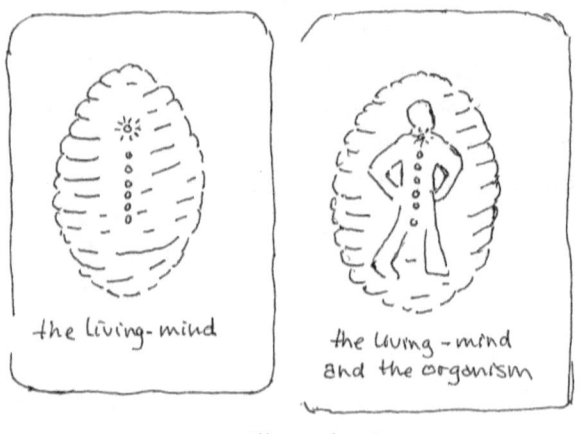

Illustration 3

3. Now as we've implied, science of course has always just assumed that our organism's *brain* was the actual source of our cognitive, and emotional abilities. That is, we have just assumed that the brain was "where our mind came from."

(For what else could we really think? Where else could we *look* for the mind... being unaware as we were of the energy body)?

But as I say, this is not really possible. Because after all, like the rest of the organism, the brain is not really alive. It is instead just a mechanism; a device, for arranging and controlling chemical interactions. It has neither volition nor "will." It's only real ability, is to react to chemicals.

4. What I'm saying is that, everything the brain does, every function that it ever performs, is only some kind of chemical reaction. A chemical reaction between the material of the brain, and chemical messengers that have been *sent* to the brain from other parts of the body (or indeed from other parts of the brain itself).

… (Actually, we say that the brain sends and receives *chemical* messages, within the body's circulatory system; and "*electrical*" messages, along the organism's nervous system. But even these "electrical messages" are really only *chemical interactions* "traveling" along the chemical structures of nerve cells.

(Anyhow…).

5. But although the brain has evolved an extremely complex and sophisticated system, for organizing and then regulating its tremendous volume of chemical interactions… nevertheless, that's really all that there is to the brain. It's just a "chemical machine" for controlling chemical processes.

So how could the brain possibly be the source of such a nonchemical phenomenon, as a living mind… that is able "to choose," and make decisions? Because the brain *has* no such abilities. It never chooses nor decides anything.

(As I say) it is really nothing more than just, a quivering mass of chemical substance; that never does anything, unless some chemical flows into it and "tells it" what to do.

6. Essentially all that the brain really is, is just a "computer." It's just a piece of hardware; no different really than an electronic device.

But instead of transistors, and diodes, and capacitors and such, it is made with chemical energy *networks*; with structures and substructures of organized and coordinated, chemical energy *processes* —which will all function in a very predetermined manner.

Chapter 4

1 So the brain is just a chemical energy *machine* —"a liquid/chemical computer."

And as such of course, it does not think; any more than a computer thinks. (Although a computer certainly *mimics* thinking). Neither is it conscious, nor aware; no mere machine is. Like any computer, all that a brain can do is to perform functions.

In fact, what the brain really does for the mind (for the energy body), is to *convert* the mind's concepts and "mental pictures" —the mind's: ideas— into forms of expression, that our person will find more usable within the context of his daily Life.

That is… into forms of expression such as: thoughts, and emotions, and sensations, etc.

2. Because you see, the mind's energy, in its natural state, dwells within what we might call: "higher forms of conception." And if perceived directly, this type of expression would just, not be very recognizable to us; let alone "usable."

(In fact, if *we were* able, to directly perceive this "higher conception" —while the mind was expressing itself— it would look to us as though our mind was just daydreaming, or "phasing out" or something. When in fact what it was really doing was simply, trying to "communicate a concept").

So how this relationship between the brain and the mind works basically, is that: as the mind experiences some form of "conception" (as I say, some "idea" or other)... this conception will actually "emanate" from the mind, as "*pulses* of living energy."

The brain, will then intercept and "assimilate" these pulses; and integrate them into its chemical processes, for "restructuring."

3. Well actually, it's not really the brain that intercepts these energy pulses from the mind.

Instead it is: two networks of "energy receptors," that are distributed throughout the physical body as an organized "energy grid" of sorts. Seers call these networks: the Intermediary Energy System.

This intermediary energy system might actually be somewhat familiar to you, through the science of *acupuncture*. Acupuncture deals with "the medical applications," *of one* of the networks of this system; which the adherents of acupuncture refer to, as the "acupuncture *meridians*."

(Seers however call this network, the mind's "*magnetic energy* receptors"; and the other network they call, the mind's "*electrical energy* receptors." We'll deal with this whole system more thoroughly in a later volume).

4. "Dimensionally speaking," seers say this energy system exists at sort of *the mid-point*... between the "dimension of luminous energies," and the "dimension of organisms."

And the primary *purpose* of this system they say, is to (magnetically, and electrically) "couple" the energy body to the organism. (In other words: *to connect the mind*... to the brain).

However, this system's primary *function*, is to "intercept and gather" the energy emissions coming from the mind; and to then conduct those emissions (in the form of energy "wave pulses") along the networks' energy pathways, to the brain's chemical systems, for restructuring.

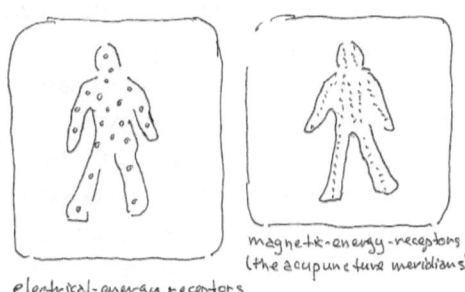

electrical-energy receptors

magnetic-energy-receptors (the acupuncture meridians)

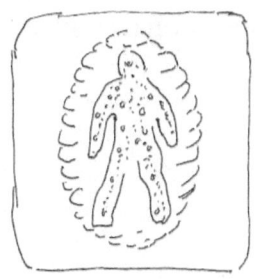

the Intermediary Energy System binds the mind to the organism

Illustration 4

So, ultimately… it is indeed *the brain's energy* that will assimilate these energy pulses coming from the mind, whenever the mind produces conception.

And then the brain uses, *its*, "networks" of chemical energy processes, to reconfigure these energy pulses.

It will shape and mold them, with its chemical energy, into a revised form of expression.

5. And this revised and reconfigured conception is then actually *returned* to the mind (as redesigned wave pulses) and reexpressed as more "firmly structured" ideas. Ideas such as (as I say): thoughts, and emotions, and perceptions; and as whatever else it is that our mind does.

What I'm saying is that, the brain simply *transforms* the mind's "diffuse" forms of higher conception, into forms of expression that will be more usable to us, as I say, within the format of our daily lives.

It just reshapes the energy of our mind's concepts, into suitable forms of *more direct* expression.

(In other words the brain is just: an energy device, in an "electrical circuit pathway"; which the wave-pulses of the mind *are sent through*... in order *to modify them*... into the "operational context" that the machine organism requires).

Chapter 5

1. But the brain is not capable of *originating* the "conception" that it converts into expression; any more than a computer would be capable of producing consciousness for itself —or than our automobile would be capable, of driving itself down to the liquor store, for a quick six-pack of *Kreuger's* fuel additive.

Because the brain is really just a chemical machine; a highly organized "chemical pulp, of dead atoms" and lifeless molecules.

As such, it could never create an expression of Life along the lines of conception. So even if we didn't know about the energy body, logic itself should tell us that there really has to be more to our mind, than just our brain.

2. In fact, science of course fully recognizes that the body is just an organized mass of nonliving, chemical substances... (atoms; molecules; even: organic cells —which are just tiny "chemical factories" really, with no actual Life inside of them).

Therefore the body (and of course the brain as well) could not really be said to actually: "be alive."

Indeed, reflecting this recognition, science does not really refer to the body as being alive. Instead it refers to the body as being simply: a living *system*; a system of nonliving material... that merely, supports, being alive.

But of course... science then goes on to attribute everything that we *do* as living creatures... *TO* the organism. Therefore, they must be assuming, that our person's consciousness and awareness are simply... *products*... of what our eyes and ears (and brain) do. (For where else, they would be thinking, could these expressions of mind be coming from)?

3. And thus, laboring under this assumption, they cannot but help to think that as living beings, we are nothing more really than just: "the sum total" of our actions.

But as we are trying to demonstrate, this is just not so. Because then of course we would just be some kind of "dead machine"; going about doing all of the things that we normally do... walking, talking, perceiving. But there would really be no "essence" inside of us. There wouldn't really be someone "there."

But as we can all testify, there is certainly more to us than being some dead machine. We are more than just the sum total: of what we do. Because as I say, there is actually "someone awake" within us. There indeed, is someone *there*.

So essentially what we're saying is that, there is not just perception; there is *a perceiver*. And there are not just thoughts; there is *a thinker* there: a "living thing" that is both conscious and aware.

And a living thing my friend, is something that a chemical machine will just never be.

4. So the whole point of course, is that the mind is not really a product of the brain… at all. I mean, how could it possibly be? Since the brain isn't really alive; and the mind is. Indeed, the mind is actually a body of living energy, which exists in and of itself.

(In fact, *that's* what's "there within us": this energy. What I mean is that, when we perceive within ourselves the part of us that indeed: is "there"… *that's* what we're perceiving. We are perceiving: "the living energies of our mind."

(So you can't really say that you don't perceive this, well… this "alleged" energy body of ours. Because you absolutely *do perceive it*; everyone does. "You" —which is to say: your mind [the part of you that you perceive, *AS* you]— *are* that body of living structured mind energy).

5. So anyway, the mind is a body of energy; a body of energy which in fact actually dwells within an entirely different "dimensional framework" altogether, from the dimension that the brain and the rest of the physical body dwell within.

And what we're really talking about here is actually, a whole dimension of "living energy"; which encompasses the entire planet (and indeed, as we will see later, the whole universe as well).

In fact, this energy occupies *the very same physical space*, as this dimension that *we* perceive; in such a way… that the energy of each dimension is actually: "operationally accessible" to the other dimension.

Seers say that this dimension of living energy, is really just a giant "group mind"… within which: all minds live together… in a symbiotic, communal effort.

Humn… (more on this later).

Chapter 6

1 Okay. So basically you could say that what we really are is a spirit, a presence, inhabiting a biological machine. This presence is a ball of living light-energy... that *uses* the organism, as a means to interact with the physical universe (because the universe is such a tremendous source of experience you see).

But as we've seen, this presence does not really inhabit the organism directly. Instead, it inhabits a body of living energy that is *coupled* to the organism's brain (and other centers of operation); and which is really just an "energy machine," for *controlling* the organism.

Actually though, seers say that this energy machine —the luminous body— is really, just a *part* of the organism. It is the brain's: "mind energy." (Though to put things in their proper perspective, seers say that the brain and the organism are really this mind energy's "physical unit").

2. Yet this luminous energy body itself (meaning: *minus* our living presence) is not intrinsically an "operational mind." As we shall be seeing, it is only what seers refer to as: the energy *machinery* of mind. It does not become an actual living mind until our living presence conjoins with its energy.

But indeed once our spirit actually does "move into

and occupy" this machine of mind-energy, the two of them will be *transformed* into a unified energy system. This energy system will then "come to Life": as a single, living mind.

3. Now while our living presence (or our spirit) is actually our "true" form of existence —that is: our true Life-form— when however it conjoins with the organism's mind energy, you might well say that a *new form of Life* has been created.

While this new form of Life is in many respects merely an expanded, or augmented form of our spirit's Life, just the same it is also a Life-form in its own right. (Seers refer to this created being —or, this living mind— as: our soul… [which *we* then simply think of, as our "person"]).

And though while it's Life is only a temporary —or mortal existence— nevertheless, seers say that within the context of this physical universe, this energy Life-form of living mind is what we really are.

We are an energy Life-form of living mind… inhabiting… a biological, machine organism.

our "spirit" is our true form of existence

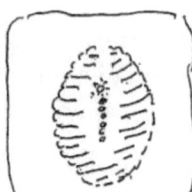
but our Life-form here in the physical-universe is our living-mind

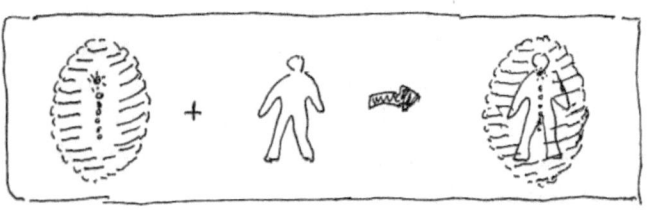

we are an energy-Life-form of living-mind, inhabiting a biological machine-organism

Illustration 5

Part Two

Chapter 7

1 Well, let's go ahead and take a closer look now at the energy structure of our mind. Now our mind, which is to say our mind's physical framework, actually consists of three, separate and distinct fields of energy.

These fields of energy provide our mind with the three basic forms of "energy expression" that all living minds are composed of.

But our mind is not just, an "energy." It is actually a living thing. So amazingly, these three energies of the mind, are separate and unique: "expressions... *of being alive.*" This is to say that, fundamentally, our mind is formed from three literal: "*states*... of being alive."

2. Well let's come at this from another direction, and simply say that, to be alive we must:

1) be conscious (that is: be awake; be responsive); we must...

2) be aware (be perceptive; be sensible of); and we must...

3) have conception (be able to conceive of; or to "imagine" —especially to be able to conceive of [or to imagine] ourself).

These are qualities shared by all living things. In fact, it is these very qualities that actually "make us alive." We are alive, *because*: we are conscious, and aware, and able to conceive of ourselves.

But don't misunderstand me. I'm not trying to say that these qualities are what a mind has "to do" in order to be alive. A mind does not as such have to ongoingly "accomplish," or bring about: being conscious, being aware, and conceiving.

What I mean is that, these three qualities of sentience are not really —well— "activities that a mind must *perform*," in order to be alive. Instead they are more like let us say: built-in *properties*, that a mind must be "constructed with."

3. In fact, our mind's consciousness, awareness, and conception are *energies*. Indeed they are literally, three separate "pools"… of *living energy* (as seers call it); each with very definite established form and structure.

So, our mind doesn't really have to ongoingly *produce* these three essential qualities of being alive. Because these qualities are *already there*, as energies; energies which manifest themselves as individual (and separate) energy *fields*.

And our mind then, is actually "built out of" these three separate pools of living energy… which is to say, these three stable fields: of living expression.

Chapter 8

1. One of these fields of living energy is a large egg-shaped structure. It actually looks like a fat football with blunt ends —"standing up" and surrounding (or "enclosing") our organism. While from the outside this field appears to be a solid mass of energy, it is really just a hollow shell, some five inches thick or so.

The material of this shell is a highly refined form of "electrical energy;" which is actually fashioned into small strands —or filaments— of a soft, white light. Seers jokingly call this luminous energy: "noodles of light;" because it's filaments actually look like flexible, fluorescent tubes of cooked spaghetti.

(However they are not quite as long as spaghetti; being only about eight inches or so in length. And actually they are thicker than spaghetti. They are about the width of cooked linguini; only they are round instead of flat.

(And really they are not tubes at all; but are instead, solid pieces of light, that only look like a "fluorescent tube," because of their soft lucidity [which is actually even softer than fluorescent light]).

2. In order to form the thickness of this egg-like, hollow energy shell, these filaments are interwoven into a "solid material." Although they are not woven in an orderly fashion, like the threads of a fabric; but instead, into very much of a jumbled mess; that for all appearances, looks quite a bit like the way that cooked spaghetti would bunch together on a plate. That is... *if*... it was only a bit more organized.

This is to say, that the material of this shell would resemble "a mess of cooked spaghetti," if only that spaghetti was oriented in more of a *linear* fashion; with the noodles basically, all running in the same direction more or less (as if they were forming the strands of a very loosely bound rope).

And to tie this image all together then let's say... that the material of this shell looks pretty much, like it is composed of: a linearly oriented, jumbled mess of fluorescent noodles, of a thick, cooked spaghetti. Well then...

our mind's living-awareness

Illustration 6

3. From one perspective, this shell is just an energy field made out of "noodles of light." But in the larger picture, it is really much more than just that. Because the energy from which this shell is composed (as we mentioned) is actually a *living* energy.

This living energy is nothing like the cold, dead chemical energy (of electrons and protons, etc.) from which physical matter is comprised.

Instead, this energy is actually a "*feeling.*" In fact, it is a "feeling energy." And what this means is that, it pretty much just sits there, "*feeling its own energy.*"

But more than this, each of the small filaments of light from which this shell is composed, actually possess the physical property of *being aware*.

4. Well really though, perhaps that's not the best way to put it. Because these filaments cannot individually be aware *OF* anything exactly. It's just that their energy merely *manifests the property* of "awareness." They are simply pieces, of "awareness energy."

So basically what we're really saying is that… the awareness shell (for so it is called) is a field of living, emotional energy… that actually produces our mind's awareness for us.

This is to say that, whenever we are in any way actually aware… *of something* or other, that's only because, our mind happens to be directly *utilizing* this awareness energy.

Seers say that this energy shell is literally, a "*living awareness*"… that *expresses* being alive, by… "feeling aware."

5. As such, it is one of the *three energy foundations* of our living mind. As a pool of unexpressed (or more exactly: undeployed) emotion, "the feeling of awareness" is essentially, just an *energy source* for our living mind.

And our mind uses this energy, to manufacture its perceptions, and feelings, and its thoughts and ideas, etc. etc. —which will then all bear (in part) the specific signature of: "feeling aware."

What I'm saying is that, this living awareness is one of the three mind energies that our "active intelligence" is built with.

As expressed intelligence, it is the part of our mind that is: "knowingly aware" of things. It is "sensible of"... the nature of the circumstances that we are currently experiencing. Something like that.

6. Can you feel this energy —this "awareness"— surrounding your body? As I say, really, it's just a feeling ... just a field, of "unexpressed emotion."

Or better actually, let's say that: it is a pool of *potential* emotion; a pool of emotional energy, just waiting to be "employed."

(And here's a clue that might help you to feel this energy: it's just an energy *shell*... that feels: "*really light*" upon the mind. [And actually, it feels "much thinner" than it really is]).

If however you are not really able, to feel this awareness surrounding your organism, then can you *feel your mind*... "being aware"? If you can feel this, what you are really doing is simply: *perceiving* this field of living awareness... while it "encloses your organism."

Because this energy field is literally the part of our mind that *manifests* awareness.

7. And F.Y.I. (for your information) seers say that for some reason, awareness is felt (and/or experienced)

exclusively from within *the left side* of the body.

Even though it may really seem to you, that you are feeling awareness in the middle of your head, a closer examination however, should reveal this feeling as actually coming from, well let's say, the left side: of "your mind" (for so it will appear).

Chapter 9

1 Okay. And so. Now residing within the empty space of what we can call, the hollow interior of the awareness shell (this space by the way is filled with what seers refer to as: "gray nether")... are six small balls of a luminous energy, which seers often call: "*the moons of consciousness*" (or sometimes: the "orbs" of consciousness).

Unlike the *white light* from which our awareness is fashioned, the highly refined "magnetic energy" from which these six "moons" are composed, is actually manifest, as light of *various* colors. In fact each of these moons is made from a different color, of a soft and mellow luminous energy. These colors are: red, orange, yellow, green, blue, and purple.

2. These moons, which are each, some two and a quarter inches in diameter, are formed into an upright column; and situated precisely *in the middle* of the awareness shell's interior.

There, they are aligned along the shell's central vertical axis, in "ascending order of frequency" (the order listed above) —with about four inches between each orb. This vertical column is then centered, upon the shell's central *horizontal* axis.

These orbs are held into this "column" through the "magnetic cohesion" they exibit; and through their interplay with the electrical field of the awareness shell. This electrical/magnetic interplay also holds them into their position, *within* the awareness shell.

Within the physical body this column's position corresponds to roughly, from just below the knees, "up the center of our body," to right about where our heart is.

3. And unlike the awareness shell, these moons of consciousness are actually well-known... in what is typically referred to as: "New Age literature." There, combined with the ball of living presence, they are known as: "the Chakras" (*chakra* [*shock*-rah] is a Sanskrit term for "wheel"), and derive their "exposure to the populace" from ancient Hindu tradition.

(On the other hand the awareness shell as I say, is less than well-known. However, it is thoroughly explored within some of the books of Carlos Castaneda; and is referenced to a much lesser degree, in some of "the Vedas" —which are very old Hindu texts.)

But even though many people are well-aware of the existence of the "moons of consciousness," most of these people have no idea at all what these moons really are. The ("New Age") literature simply refers to them as "energy centers" —that allegedly: "supply a special energy" to certain parts of the body.

(Which actually is *sort of* true —after a fashion [meaning: that's one of the things that they *also do* (and as I say)... sort of]).

4. Further, they believe these "energy centers" to actually be: "within the organism itself"; forming an equally spaced vertical alignment along the spinal column —from the base of the spine, up to the head. (And the living presence they envision, as actually hovering *above* the head).

However, seers who are able to directly perceive these "moons" (able that is to "physically" *view* them) will attest, that they don't actually exist within the organism at all —but instead as we have pointed out, within the interior of the awareness shell.

(And incidentally, referring to them as residing "within the organism," is merely how seers used to *allude* to them, while conversing with "the general populace").

Our mind's living-consciousness

Illustration 7

5. Like awareness, our consciousness energy is a pool of *feeling* (meaning that: it "sits there, feeling its own energy"). Indeed seers refer to it as: "the feeling of consciousness." But make no mistake. I'm not saying that this energy merely… "feels like"… it is being conscious.

What I am saying is that, the only reason at all that

our mind even *exhibits* "consciousness," is because this energy is there... *expressing consciousness*. As I say, these small balls of luminous "feeling energy"... indeed, *ARE*... our mind's consciousness!

You might think that you're conscious (or: awake), simply because you've got your eyes open. But this is just not so. Your mind experiences itself being awake, because these six orbs of luminous energy are there... actually, *being* awake!

(And your mind *is aware* that you are awake... because, the egg-like luminous energy field that is surrounding your organism, is aware of that).

6. But, the trait of "consciousness," is not the only contribution that this energy provides our mind.

These "conscious orbs" are also a field of what you might call "available energy"; which (as it does with our awareness) our mind utilizes as an energy source, for creating various applications of active intelligence (as I say such as: perceptions, emotions, thoughts, etc.).

In fact, *as* available energy, this field is basically, just six different "frequencies" —which is to say: six different "levels of intensity"— *of the condition* of "being awake." (Or you might just say that these orbs are really: six different "*levels of consciousness*").

When combined with the energies of our awareness and our conception, they provide our mind with the source to assemble "any frequency" (meaning: any *type*) of cognitive, emotional, or perceptual expression that our mind requires.

(For instance, your mind might need to combine a blue, or even a purple intensity of consciousness, with a corresponding, "depth" of awareness energy, and a correlative "viscosity" of conception energy, in order to comprehend a difficult concept in mathematics.

(But you might need only a yellow, or an orange consciousness [or maybe, something like a goldish blend, you see], to decide whether to go to the beach, or whether to go play mini-golf).

7. As such then, the moons of consciousness are simply another of "the three energy foundations" from which our living mind is built. To put it in a word, this field of energy is actually: a "*living consciousness*"; that provides our mind (as I say), with six different *degrees* of being awake.

And F.Y.I. once again, seers say that consciousness, as the perfect corollary of awareness, is "felt" —that is: experienced— exclusively (for some reason or other) upon *the right side* of the body.

Chapter 10

1 The third energy base that our mind is composed of, as we've seen, is our living presence. Its "field" is actually: a highly refined form of "electromagnetic energy."

Now while our mind's two emotional energies are softly luminous, our living presence on the other hand, is actually, a very brightly intense, white-light energy. More than anything else really, it resembles a tiny white sun.

This living presence is about the size of a small apple (or a fairly large plum [say about some two and three quarters inches in diameter]). Like the moons of consciousness, it is of course also situated within the hollow interior of the awareness shell.

In fact just like consciousness, it is also aligned along the shell's central vertical axis —some ten or eleven inches above the uppermost "moon." In the physical body this corresponds to the region of our larynx (or our "Adam's apple").

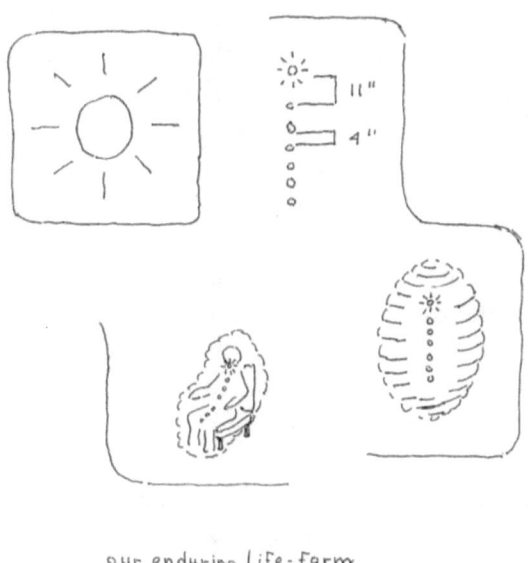

our enduring Life-form

Illustration 8

2. Now as emotional energies, our consciousness and awareness are actually just *feelings* within us. Our living presence however is really more of an "idea" in our mind, than it is a feeling. This is to say, that it's really more of a "thought energy," than it is a feeling energy.

Actually, our living presence is basically just: "a concept." In fact, seers say that this presence is really an ongoing and continuous, *state* of conceptualizing. In our mind this state is manifest as: the conception of being alive —which you could really call, "the *active* form of presence."

The essential quality of our living presence is that, it ceaselessly, "conceives-itself into being."

3. So as I say, presence is more of an idea than it is a

feeling. Indeed seers often refer to it as simply: "the idea of being alive." And they say that the two "processes" then that make us alive are:

1) *the feeling*-of-being-alive (provided by our two luminous energies); and...

2) *the idea*-of-being-alive (which is provided by the energy of our living presence).

Or in more practical terms seers say, that what "we do" to make ourselves alive is that… we feel, and we "imagine"… (because as we shall be seeing, the idea of being alive is really: the actualized *process*, of "imagining that we are alive").

4. Even though this energy of presence is actually our "immortal" spirit (meaning that it is essentially our "true Life-form"); nevertheless, its function within our living mind is really no different than that of the two mortal energies, our consciousness and our awareness. It is simply, just one of the energy sources that our mind is composed of.

It's just a pool of imagining energy, that our mind is able to use —in conjunction with its energy pool of being conscious and its energy pool of being aware— to construct our mind's cognitive, emotional, and perceptual processes.

And as we've already suggested, and shall be thoroughly exploring a little later on, *how* our mind goes about building these processes of expression, is by *combining* its three sentient energies into various ratios, and mixtures and such.

This of course will depend upon what the desired expression calls for… so much: "responsiveness to"; so much: "sensibility of"; and so much: "imagining."

5. And F.Y.I. seers say that conception is (seemingly) expressed *in the organism*, sort of: "in the middle of our head"; which simply means that's where it seems to our brain, that conception is coming from.

And perhaps we should pause here a moment to examine what that really means… to say that: it seems "to the brain" (that conception takes place in the middle of the head). Because of course we've taken some pains to establish that our brain is not actually "alive."

Nevertheless down through the ages, the brain has evolved as literally *a function* of the mind. This is to say, that it has developed itself into a tool, for assisting the mind in its endeavors.

And one of the things that the mind wants to do —at least, until our person has reached a given level of "development"— is to be absolutely convinced: that *the organism* is "who the mind really is." So one of the brain's evolved functions, is to do everything that it can to keep the mind thinking that.

6. Therefore the brain actually "tells the mind" things like: "conception takes place in the head" (in the brain you see) rather than: within a ball of intense white light, hovering there, in the vicinity of the Adam's apple.

And the brain will also tell the mind that: your consciousness and your awareness actually take place, respectively: "on the right side and the left side, *of your person*." This implies of course that they are taking place upon the left and right sides (as it were), of *your brain* —rather than: within two luminous energy fields, coexisting within the same physical space as your organism... though in a *dimensional variant* of that space all their own. (Okay...).

And these of course are not really thoughts that the brain has. They are instead, "chemical pathways" that the brain develops, during the course of its evolution; that produce these kinds of, "axillary ideas" within the mind... as the situation calls for it.

7. So as I say... even though this field of energy, our living presence, is our "enduring form of existence"; nevertheless, the expression of conceptualizing that it brings to our mind, is really no more important to being alive, than being conscious and being aware are (which of course are merely our "mortal" expressions of mind).

Really our spirit's conception of itself, is just *one* of the three properties of sentience that are necessary, to be alive here in the physical universe, as an organic being, with a living mind.

Chapter 11

1 But in order to better understand how our mind's three sentient energies actually *work together*, let's switch our tactics a little bit here. Let's put all of this into more of a perspective, of examining what the essential *differences* are, between our luminous energies and our living presence.

And let us first consider: our two luminous energies.

Now grandiose as it may sound, seers actually refer to the two feelings generated by our luminous energies, our consciousness and awareness, as the literal: "*substance of Life.*"

And it is this "emotional substance" they say, that being alive is constructed from. In other words, being conscious and being aware are the literal *media* —or: "material"— that our Life is put together with.

2. Indeed seers say that these expressions are the two: "feelings of being alive in the physical universe," that comprise *the very foundation* of our mind's existence.

Right this very minute, in spite of whatever else we might happen to be involved in, what our mind is *really* doing (that is, what it is predominately "focused upon") is going about: being conscious and being aware.

Because… that of course, is how we are *enacting* being alive. That's how we are "bringing it about": by *being* conscious; and by being *aware*. (And of course [as we'll be momentarily discussing] by then realizing, that indeed *we are* conscious and aware).

So what I'm really trying to say here is that, these two feelings, or activities, are the literal "substances," that *our mind* is actually, "putting itself together with" (ongoingly, moment by moment).

Indeed you might even well say, that *abiding within* these two feelings, is actually *the bulk,* of what our mind goes around doing.

3. The conception of being alive (on the other hand) is what seers call: the *essence* of Life. Although it is the part of our mind that is sort of "behind the scenes" —or in the background— nonetheless, it is Life's true and actual source.

You might say that it is the "idea" that *empowers* being conscious and being aware. In other words, being conscious (for instance) wouldn't really amount to much, unless we actually *realized* that we were being conscious. That is, unless we actually had some sort of "conception of ourself," going around *being* conscious.

And for the most part, that's the main thing that our conception (of being alive) actually *does* for our mind. It allows our mind to realize (that is: to conceive) that indeed, *it is* conscious and aware.

4. Well rather than it being merely a conception "of being alive," seers say that this energy is more exactly: a conception "of its own existence" (meaning, that it is: a conception, *of itself* being alive).

And they then refer to this "conception of itself" as: our "immortal" essence. They say (as we've already begun examining) that this "immortal essence" is an actual "spirit," that comes to this physical universe from its own dimension of existence.

It comes here they say in order *to enhance* its Life situation; through the experience of being alive as an emotional being. (Which experience it is able to bring about, by *temporarily inhabiting* the sentient feelings of being conscious and being aware).

5. And the main reason really that seers refer to this conception as: "immortal" is because… once our spirit has undergone this, "detour" into the physical (and emotional) realm… it then simply *returns to*, from where it has come. In other words it's Life span, is *not dependent* upon the organism.

However, in sharp contrast to this, the two *feelings* of being alive, (our consciousness and awareness), absolutely *are*, immutably tied into the organism's existence. As such they are thus, quite mortal indeed.

In fact seers are able to witness, that when the organism "dies," our awareness shell will sort of shrivel up and wither away; it's energy presumably returning to "it's source."

And the energy orbs of our consciousness, in a somewhat similar fashion, will lose their magnetic cohesion, and sort of "crumble away" within an hour or so of the organism's demise; their energy also presumably returning to its source.

Part Three

Chapter 12

1 Seers say that in the strictest sense what our luminous energies really are (in league of course with their organism, and its eyes and ears and nose, etc.)… or this is just another way of saying that, what our body (and its intrinsic mind energ*y*) really is… is literally, a *perception machine*... which is able to ongoingly create: a perception of itself, and a perception of its environment.

But perception alone is not enough to build a living mind. A mind must really be able to "*translate*" its perception into some form of reality; or nothing would have any meaning for the mind. The mind would be a complete "blank."

2. If you raised your hand, put it in front of your eyes and stared at it... you could stare, and stare, and stare. But unless your "conception of things" stepped in to explain what was actually happening, you would have absolutely no concept of what that hand was. Nor indeed would you have any concept of what *you* were; nor in fact even that: "you were staring at your hand."

You would have no conception at all: only an inert, and ineffective consciousness; and a rather vague, and ill-defined awareness of sorts. In a way, you would only be like some kind of recording device; like say a "smart camera" or something like that.

3. So what our consciousness and awareness really are (in league as I say with our brain and its organism) are just two energy masses of "living perception"; that more or less are just "standing there" as *a potential*, for allowing our spirit to experience being conscious and being aware.

And how our spirit is able to actually *realize* this potential, is by using the perception that these two living energies create... *as a means*... for *becoming* "conscious of ourselves," and (becoming) "aware of our environment."

In other words, we become conscious of ourselves and aware of our environment, by actually: *perceiving* ourselves and our environment.

4. You see, perception is continuously transpiring within these two living energies (ongoingly) simply as an inherent condition of their energy —and of course, of that energy's incorporation, within an organism possessing eyes and ears, etc. But, as we were just considering, it's sort of a "blank" perception; because there is no conception *of what* they are perceiving.

Essentially, these energies are just two living "machines," that each have the ability to assemble perception (to assemble: a perception of ourself; and a perception of our environment); but *not* the ability, to comprehend that this is what they are doing.

But once our living presence actually ("comes down" and) "plugs into" this perception machine (meaning, when our spirit is born into this world) and combines its conception energy *with* the organism's consciousness and awareness energies... then the perception machine will "come alive"; and be able to assemble perception within the boundaries of "active intelligence."

And what this means simply is that: as you go about perceiving, you will also, understand *what you are perceiving*.

5. (And this is all pretty much, the manner in which the luminous energies also produce, consciousness and awareness. I mean, they produce consciousness and awareness strictly *as a condition* of their living energy. But as I say, they are really unable to comprehend that they are doing this.

(But once our spirit [as I say: "comes down" and] lends its "conception of itself," *to* this consciousness and awareness, then "the whole mind" emerges, as a *sentient entity*: who is not only conscious and aware, but who also *realizes* that it is conscious and aware).

6. And so then, as we become thus "fully immersed" in our perception, our Life begins taking place as a living mind that is both conscious and aware.

Indeed seers often equate Life *with* perception. They say that what Life really is… is simply: "a state of *ongoing* perception" (and meaning of course: "true" perception… wherein, not only are we conscious that we are perceiving; but we are aware, of *what* we are perceiving). In other words, we are alive, essentially, *as a product* of our perception.

But not (as we pointed out at the beginning of this text) as a *direct* product of perception. Instead seers say that fundamentally, perceiving *indirectly* makes us alive: by providing us "with *the opportunity*" to bring our Life about… "*within the arena*… of perception."

What I'm saying is that perception is merely, the activity, that brings consciousness and awareness... "into play." I mean it simply gives our consciousness and awareness, a means —or: a *venue*— within which *to create* being conscious and being aware.

7. What this really means is that, *AS*: "we go about perceiving," we become *conscious* of ourselves (we become conscious you see that: "well... *here we are... perceiving*"). And we become *aware*, of what it is that *we are* perceiving ("oh, here I am perceiving: *my surroundings*").

And of course, what actually "consummates" this: being conscious of ourselves, and aware of what we are perceiving, is when our spirit: "completes our perception", by: "imagining *our participation*" in these events.

Chapter 13

1 So basically being alive is assembled within us, from three fundamental states of passive —or benign— sentience. And while each of them are indeed... *living* states of expression... nonetheless, the basic purpose they serve... is being merely, the independent *components* of Life.

In other words, our mind is put together with three separate and distinct *pieces*: of "living expression"; each of which bring a very specific, and unique process to our mind. Just the same though, these pieces of our living mind are really only *energies*; whose beneficial contribution to "being alive," is their energy properties.

2. You see, our consciousness, taken by itself, doesn't really do anything but to just "sit there" and "be conscious." And our living awareness likewise, can only sit there "being aware." And by the same token our living presence —who though indeed is our "immortal" form of existence— can really do nothing but to sit and "imagine itself." And that's all that these energies do. That's all that they *can do*!

Because independently of each other —or what I mean is, outside of their union as our living mind— all that they really are basically (as I say) is just: energies, you see. Energies with given characteristic "properties." Just three separate and distinctive *pools*, of "the three required energies of being alive."

3. (You might think that our spirit would be a special circumstance. Because unlike our consciousness and awareness [who are alive, as a consequence really, of the organism's Life] our spirit of course is actually, "already alive"... *exclusive* of the organism.

(Nevertheless, at our spirit's most basic level of existence, that's all that it really is: just "an energy" whose unique property is "to conceive" —or: "to imagine."

(And for our purposes here, you might well say, that until it is "plugged into" our mind's perception machine —and is then able to perceive our person and our environment— our spirit really has nothing [outside of the bare fact of its own existence] to conceive *of*.

(Therefore basically, like the two mortal energies, it is just a "pool" of its own energy property; just a pool of conception *energy*).

4. However, put these three energies together, under circumstances wherein they are compelled to begin interacting with each other (like: struggling together, to exist as an organism, in a physical environment)... and... *poof!*... these passive energies will essentially, magically transform themselves, into a thriving little "ecosystem" of ongoing Life; which we then call: our living mind.

But how does this process come about really? What I mean is, where do these living energies actually come from? And how are they able to get together in order to form themselves into a living mind?

Well... at this early stage of our narrative, being able to address ourselves to these questions, with any degree of thoroughness, would prove to be somewhat beyond our means. (Because that discussion will require a great deal of information, which we simply haven't had the opportunity to examine yet). Nevertheless, I think that we should at least provide ourselves with a basic *sketch* of these things for now.

5. So if you would, let us begin by taking a brief look at our living presence; the real source you might well say, of our being alive.

Now, as we have just been intimating, examining where our living presence (that is, our spirit) actually comes from, would be a rather lengthy and involved process. And this is really not the best place to begin such an elaboration. (But we *will definitely* get to this topic).

But, it should serve our purposes well-enough for now, to say that our living presence comes from the realm… "where spirits dwell." (And as we shall come to discover, this is an energy domain existing in an altogether different "dimension" actually, from this physical universe).

6. Now while indeed it is really our "true form of existence," our spirit nonetheless is nothing more than just an energy of "presence."

And as having no more existence than just "being a presence" is as you might well imagine, pretty much the "light" version of being alive… seers say (as we've suggested) that our spirit enhances its existence, by "coming from its domain," and temporarily conjoining with the mortal consciousness and awareness energies, in order to create a "whole, living mind."

Together, these mortal energies are basically just a single "living machine," that the universe apparently has evolved for this very purpose.

7. And this union with these luminous energies will then greatly enrich our spirit's Life experiences, you see; by expanding its simple state of just "being there" ("being present")… into the ongoing processes of also: being *conscious* "of being there"; and being aware, of *being* "conscious of being there."

And this of course all within the format: of being alive as an emotional being, in a physical universe.

Chapter 14

1. Actually our luminous energy body, otherwise known as: our organism's mind energy, is constructed to be the perfect instrument for our spirit to inhabit.

Because if you took the electromagnetic energy that our spirit's living presence is composed of, and separated it, into what would effectivelely be... its constituent components... what you would actually get would be, a magnetic, consciousness like energy... and an electrical awareness like energy.

In other words, "consciousness and awareness," are essentially, what the energy of "presence" is composed of really. (Presence is sort of: "being aware, of being conscious").

2. So basically, our mind's luminous body consists of quantities, of the two constituent energies of "being present." And these energies are collected, into two relatively large (and separate) "pools" of luminous energy —in *much larger volumes* you see, than they are found in our living presence.

They are then made available to our living presence, as sort of: "energy tools for assembling experience."

And of course (let's put it that) the first thing our living presence *does* with these energies... is to utilize them to produce a living mind. She then uses this mind for interacting with the physical universe —in order to provide her as I say, with opportunities for enhancing her existence.

3. (Well, I suppose we'd better pause to mention that, as you probably noticed, I have just begun referring to our living presence in the feminine: as "she," and "her." So understandably you're wondering: what's going on with that?

(But please let me assure you, that this is in no way any kind "of affectation."

(It's simply that, seers claim all spirits really are fundamentally: "female." Therefore, referring to them —that is, referring to our living presence— in the feminine gender, far from being an affectation… is actually the proper thing to do.

(Well then. So anyhow, back to our story…).

4. Okay. So our spirit comes from her dimension, in order to inhabit the body of luminous mind energies.

But *how about* these luminous energies that our spirit inhabits? Where *do they* come from? What I mean is, how do these energies really come about? And how is our spirit actually *able* to conjoin with them? And of course, how does this all tie in with the organism?

5. Well… while the organism is developing within the mother's womb, the two mortal energy fields of the organism's mind energy, its consciousness and its awareness energies, are developing "right alongside of it."

Now where these energies actually come from —or more to the point: where they "derive their source"— is from two universe size pools of living energy; one of which is actually a *Living Consciousness*, and the other which is a *Living Awareness*.

Where these pools of living energy actually exist, is *right here*, all around us. Indeed, as we mentioned earlier, they occupy the very same space the physical universe does. Although as we shall be examining, they occupy this space, in a "dimensional reality" all their own.

6. (Even though we earlier referred to "living energy" as coming from: "a dimension of its own," actually as we shall be thoroughly exploring, instead of but a *single* dimension, there are in fact these *two* dimensions. One is a dimension of consciousness energy, and the other, of awareness energy.

(And indeed there is a third dimension as well, made entirely of "presence" energy. But it doesn't really exist: here "all around us," like the other two dimensions do. Instead, it exists in a much different type of reality. [We'll be looking into this]).

7. What these immense pools of living energy really are seers say, are the two "mortal" mind energies of the great *Spirit*, who ceaselessly: "dreams all Life in the universe, into its ongoing state of existence." In other words, they are the mortal mind energies, of the Living Spirit whom most of us would simply refer to, as "God."

However... let us leave the exploration of these two dimensions of living energy to a later time. Let us instead continue to focus upon the development of *our mind's* "energy body."

Chapter 15

1 Now during this primal stage of the organism's development, the two "evolving fields" of the brain's mortal mind energy, could not exactly be called: *living* energies. What I mean is, that they do not yet possess consciousness and awareness; but are still developing the ability to do so. Actually all that they really are at this point you might say, is just inert "forces."

In fact at this stage of their development, not only are these forces not really living energies, but they don't even exist as recognizable "fields" as of yet. They are just sort of: "loosely arranged forces, *in proximity* with the organism."

2. Nonetheless, at some point well-along in our fetus' development, these forces will finally coalesce into fully completed field structures. In other words they will develop into fully formed *fields* of inert (that is: "inactive") mind energy.

(This is to say, they will have completely formed themselves into the luminous body's overt structure [the structure seen in illustration # 2]; but, as I say, will still not quite yet be living energies).

And when these two fields then finally *become* fully developed, their energy will actually begin exerting: a low intensity, attractive force… which will *bind* these two fields, *to* each other, and to the intermediary energy system of the organism.

3. And not only this but, this force will also begin exerting a pressure, upon "the dimensional barrier" that separates the two dimensions of luminous energy, from the dimension where living presence resides. And this pressure will be powerful enough to actually produce a "dimensional rift" (a "rip") in this modest barrier separating the dimensions.

(This almost sounds like science fiction. But it will all become very mundane, once we begin thoroughly exploring these "dimensions of living energy").

And this "rift," or "opening" between dimensions, will allow the attractive force being exerted by these luminous energies, to "reach into" the dimension of living presence; and to literally *pull* our spirit… "across," and *into* (what then becomes) the energy body.

4. And it's really as simple as that. Although how "the energy" of the whole thing actually comes about —causing our presence to be accessible, well, to *this particular* developing organism— is something that we will cover later.

(We might mention here, that this dimension of living presence [or: the "Living Ocean," as It is called] is essentially just a pool of "available presences" —or spirits— who are all just sort of "hovering there"; while going about: conceiving of their own existence).

5. So when our spirit has been pulled from its own dimension, through this dimensional rift, and it is pulled *into* the energy body… the first thing that will happen, is that the intense white light that our spirit's energy emits, will "flood into" the emotional energies, and "illuminate them."

Now seers say that what this light really is, is the energy produced as our spirit goes about conceiving of its own existence. Consequently, seers call this light simply: "the light of conception."

Or indeed, more formally they call this light: "the light *of Life*." Because conceiving of your existence —that is, "imagining" that you're alive— is really *the very essence* of Life you see.

6. So the two emotional energies will then *absorb* this light of Life that our spirit is emitting; and become for the first time actually "luminous."

(Well really though, once these luminous energies have completed the formation of their field structures —but *before* the spirit is pulled into them— they emit sort of a very weak, low-level light.

(But this light is really nothing as bright as the mellow luminosity that they exhibit, once the light of conception floods into them).

7. However, even at this late stage of their development —once their field structures have already formed; and begun exerting the attractive force needed to capture a living presence— as the light of conception then begins flooding into them for the first time… these two fields of mortal mind energy could still not really be called, states of *living* expression.

What I mean is that they are not really "alive" yet. At this point their energy still only has, *the potential* for Life.

Chapter 16

1 Now in the delicate world of living energies, the light from our living presence is actually an emanating *force*.

As such then, as it floods into the two fields of potential Life, the force of that light will actually start "pushing those energies around"; causing them to start "churning, and turning over" —like a car motor turns over, when you turn the key.

In other words, being flooded with this light of conception, is what actually "starts these energies up." It brings them to Life, by sort of jump-starting them. It gets them started "vibrating, and humming." And then they "give a jerk," and start working. They become operational.

(Actually once operational these energies literally *do* "hum," with a very low-pitched vibration, sort of like: "a-a-u-u-m-m-m." And some seers, after years of training themselves to sit quietly and listen for this sound, are actually able to perceive it).

2. However, though this light is the energy being emanated from ongoing *conception* (from our spirit, *conceiving* of being alive), it does not cause the two luminous energies to also "have conception." Because having conception is just not what these energies do.

But it does cause them to begin manifesting *their own* energy characteristics.

This is to say, when the energy of conception begins flooding into these two fields of mind energy, they will instantly "come to Life" —because that's what they were sitting there waiting to do. They come to Life, by beginning to express the sentient properties of *their* respective energies —meaning: consciousness and awareness.

And this means that, these two mortal energies will become (respectively): conscious, and aware. And as such then… they will actually begin emanating: the "light of consciousness" and "light of awareness."

3. Now as we've seen, these two luminous energies are actually *emotional* energies. And what this is really saying of course, is that these energies are "feelings." In other words that's how these energies literally "perform being alive": they *feel*. (They produce the state of: "Life being experienced… as a feeling").

Okay. So our consciousness and awareness energies come to Life, by beginning to produce feeling within themselves. That is, they begin to feel conscious and to feel aware. But does this burgeoning feeling within our two luminous energies, actually make *the organism* "alive"? Well no; not quite yet.

Because, even though our mind will now have *the potential* to experience consciousness and awareness (as a feeling); it really does not as of yet, have anyone capable of "employing those experiences." That is, it does not have anyone capable, *of being* conscious and aware.

And of course who we're talking about is our spirit.

4. In other words, in spite of basically "possessing" both consciousness, and awareness (well, possessing them as two pools of luminous feeling), our organism isn't exactly alive yet. Because it doesn't really have someone "driving" our consciousness and awareness. What I'm saying is that, our spirit (our conception) is not yet: "in possession" of the mind.

And what this really means is that, even though our spirit has already been *pulled into* this dimension… the process is not quite complete. Because our spirit has not yet "fully awakened" into this world you see.

So consequently, she is really in no condition to begin assuming an active role as part of a living mind. In order to become so, she must first as I say: "be awakened."

And so, what will then actually bring our spirit's "awakening" *about*… are the two luminous feelings; that have themselves just been "awakened into expression," by the light of conception.

5. Okay. So as the two mortal energies then begin producing feeling (or actually we should really say, as they begin *expressing* feeling), this feeling —as an energy— will begin "emanating into the interior" of the energy body.

And you might say that essentially, it will actually "beset" our spirit's energy —assailing it; pushing up against it as a constant pressure (the pressure you see, of feeling: *being expressed*).

And this is pretty much what our spirit's energy has just done to the two luminous energies. It has "pushed into them" and actually brought them to Life —by *impelling* their energy to begin producing feeling (which of course is the "characteristic ability" of those two energies).

6. So this feeling (as an expressed energy [and seers define energy as simply, "a pressure" —meaning: a force that has *progressed*, from being merely a potential *to create* pressure (of some kind); into being an "energy," that is now "pushing *against*" something (or "*pulling* against" something)]... but this feeling [as an expressed energy]) will push back *into our spirit's* energy, as a "pressure."

And it will serve as a catalyst —not for bringing our spirit to Life (because she is already alive)— but for "shaking her out of her slumber," as it were.

In other words our spirit "will awaken into this world," by becoming aware of the two feelings that are pressing up against her, and "disturbing her energy." And she will immediately begin *exploring* these two feelings (as we will shortly be examining) by trying to "interface" with her consciousness and awareness.

And at this point we can say, that "the Life process" within the organism has begun.

Part Four

Chapter 17

1 Well okay, that's the basic outline. But it would probably be to our advantage to take a closer look at this process. Because there are a couple of things here that we really need to grasp.

That is... if we want to understand, later in this narrative, how the living energies *of our environment* work; and how they are able to coerce our mind, into, well let us say: "an interactive complicity," with the environment's group-operation. (Well *that* sounds just a bit ominous).

And the first thing that we might want to look at is: how the feelings of consciousness and awareness are actually *able* to push up against the energy of our living presence. I mean, what's the mechanics behind this process?

2. Well it's no big deal really. You see feeling is what seers refer to, as an *applied* force. What this means is that, as an energy, feeling is actually *doing* something. And what it is doing is... *manifesting* itself. It is manifesting itself, *AS* "feeling" you see.

And as energies in this sort of circumstance will tend to do, as feeling is manifesting itself (that is: as it is being expressed) it creates a *secondary field* around itself; as an *effect* you see, of its activity as an energy.

What I mean is that, as feeling is being expressed, its energy actually "radiates outwards," beyond the confines of its source —very much like a household oven; which as "an effect" of energizing its coil (that is: its heating element) creates a "field" of radiating heat around that coil, which you can feel some distance away.

And that's pretty much what our luminous energies are doing as well. They are emitting a field of radiating feeling around themselves… as an active by-product, of producing being conscious and being aware *within* their feeling energies.

3. Well rather than comparing feeling to a heat, that simply radiates off into empty space, seers say that feeling is really something more along the lines, of a simple "emanation" (than it is a strict radiation).

Because it never really "escapes" it's source; but remains you might say, "attached" to that source as an encircling field of energy (very much like the magnetic field produced in a magnet).

So what's really going on here then, is that, as an energy effect of ongoingly expressing consciousness and awareness, these luminous energies will actually produce, respectively: a secondary *magnetic* field of "emanating feelings"; and, a secondary *electrical* field of emanating feelings… which will then each surround the luminous energy that is generating them.

4. So as I say, these fields are the consequent "energy emanations," *of the feeling* that is being "generated" at the moment, within the luminous energies. If the luminous energies generate: *joy*, then their secondary fields will actually *emanate* that "joy" you see.

Okay. Now our consciousness and awareness energies are basically, fixed, stable, and immutable: "things, in and of themselves." However, these two secondary fields "encircling" our consciousness and awareness, in stark contrast to this, are *highly* mutable, vacillating fields of radiating feelings.

And like I say, rather than simply radiating off into empty space (like heat would), these two emanating energies erect themselves, into these fluctuating fields of what seers call: "reciprocating wave pulses." (Tiny pulses that are continuously: pushing out and then pulling back in; out and back in; out and back in…).

You might say that these fields surround each of the luminous energies, somewhat like a slightly pulsing "glow." In fact that's what seers call them: *glows*.

5. Well really though, it's not totally accurate to say that these "glows" actually "surround" the two fields of luminous energy; although they are usually referred to in that manner… that is, as "encircling fields."

Because, while the glow of consciousness indeed, actually *does* "surround and encircle" the orbs of consciousness, the glow of awareness on the other hand, is basically emanated only into *the interior* of the awareness shell —and does not as such, "encircle its exterior."

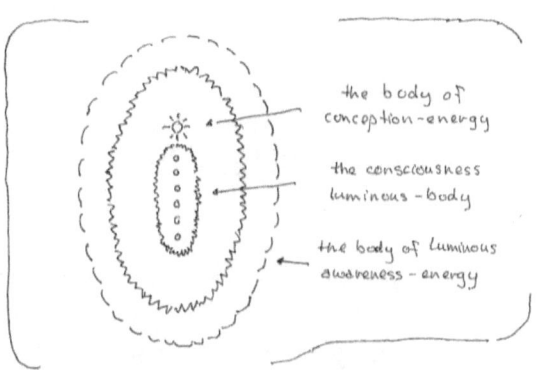

the glow-of-awareness emanating within the awareness-shell, and enveloping the ball of conception

the glow-of-consciousness emanating around the consciousness-orbs, and also enveloping the ball of conception

Illustration 9

6. So as I say, these glows are the energy product of "the applications of mind" that our luminous energies are producing. But how do these glows really fit into all of this? Because what we're trying to explore here is: how the luminous energies are able, to *push up against* our living presence.

And how in fact they *are* able to do this, is through these glows.

What I mean is that, it is actually these emanating fields of reciprocating wave pulses that will push up against our spirit's energy (with *the force*, you see, of "expressed feeling"); essentially, compelling her to perceive them.

So what this means actually is that, our spirit doesn't really perceive the two luminous energies directly. Instead, she perceives their "glows."

Chapter 18

1. And not only do these glows merely allow our spirit, to actually *become aware* of the two luminous energies. But they also allow her to become aware, of precisely what these energies are actually "*feeling.*"

What I'm saying is that, essentially, these glows will "impart" to our spirit, what the luminous energies "are doing" on a cognitive, emotional, and perceptual level.

But in order to understand how this works, let us first examine a little more closely how exactly these glows come about.

2. Well as we know, the most basic applications of mind that our luminous energies produce are: "the feeling of being conscious," and "the feeling of being aware." And one of the things we need to understand about these two feelings, is that they exist within a condition of "constant fluctuation."

What this means is that, the feelings of consciousness and of awareness are always changing (that is: altering themselves)... *slightly*... as a result of our mind's ongoing activity.

This however is strictly an "internal" energy event so to speak. It's merely a change in what these energies "are doing"; and in no way really affects the energy structures of the two luminous fields.

Alright. But why are these ongoing fluctuations in our luminous energies significant?

3. Well… these luminous feelings, as we've mentioned, along of course with our living presence, are actually the "energy foundations" of our living mind.

Between the three of them, they supply our mind with the entire resource that it uses, *to create* our thoughts and emotions (and perceptions, and states of mind, etc. etc.).

And whenever we create these thoughts and emotions and such things, how we go about making this happen, is by using our conception "*as a tool*," to actually *modify*, some of the energy, of our feeling conscious, and of our feeling aware… *into* these thoughts, and emotions, and perceptions, etc.

(And this by the way is why seers claim that everything the mind does, is an expression of some type of "feeling." That's because everything the mind does, is literally *assembled* from feeling energy).

4. We'll examine more thoroughly how this all works as we go along.

But for now what we need to know is that, whenever we modify some of the energy of our luminous feelings —to create our thoughts and emotions— this will actually slightly alter *some*, of the basic "energy configurations" of consciousness and awareness… *while* we are thinking that thought, or feeling that emotion, or experiencing that perception.

In other words, *how* we are being conscious and how we are being aware, changes just a little bit.

So… as the luminous energies are altered —through the activity of creating our thoughts and feelings, etc.— this is significant to the mind's operation, because these alterations will of course cause their "glows," to *also* change.

5. What I'm saying is that, as our consciousness and awareness are *transfigured* by our thoughts and such, the energy activity within these two luminous energies, will create "corresponding" changes within their *glows*.

In other words, because these glows are really just *emanations* from the energies of our consciousness and awareness… the wave configurations and "frequencies" of these emanations will be continuously "revised and remodeled," by the ongoing energy activity of creating our thoughts and feelings, *within* consciousness and awareness.

And this of course is the process that "shapes" these glows, into ongoingly "*emulating*" the feelings, that the luminous energies are producing.

6. But whereas the alterations of the luminous energies are actually *very slight* changes, the permutations within their glows however, are really of a much more radical nature; involving essentially, the continuous (and pretty much: "wildly") shaping, and re-shaping, of their *entire field* of emanations.

But because the pulses of these glows are in fact so minute, these changes in the shapes of their glow *fields*, will actually take place within, relatively, very narrow margins.

In other words, if you were *to watch* these two glowing energy fields, their general over-all appearance wouldn't really change very much. They would simply look like they were only "shivering"; or like they were merely "vibrating."

Chapter 19

1. But the relevant feature for us in all of this, is that it is actually these fluctuations within the glows of the luminous energies, that make it possible for our living presence to be able *to perceive*, what our consciousness and awareness energies "are up to." (And this understandably, is a very important function of the mind).

So let's see how this works.

2. Now as I say what these glows really are, is tiny emanating *pulses* of "feeling." And what this actually implies (being "pulses"... of: *feeling*) is that: they are indubitably, the energy product, of *transpiring Life*. Because feeling of course (and especially *pulsing* feeling) is undeniably, *an expression* of being alive.

Indeed, these glows are literally, the manifestation: of consciousness being conscious, and of awareness being aware.

Now... being the emanations of "Life *taking place*," these glows, as we've implied, are "a reflection", of *the sentient activity* that is occurring, *within* the two luminous energies —as they go about being conscious and being aware.

Or, how I would really like to phrase this is: you might say that, within their "feeling," these glows actually "*carry the image*," of what consciousness and awareness are doing (that is, of whatever "ideas" they are experiencing; or, whatever "emotions" they are undergoing; or indeed, what they are perceiving; etc. etc.).

3. We've referred to these "residual glows" as tiny wave pulses of feeling. But from a more practical point of view we could really refer to them as basically just: *energy vibrations*... vibrations of a very subtle and refined nature, which as I say more or less "carry" —or convey— the state of mind that produces them.

What this all means effectively is that: because they are produced by sentient energies, if you happened *to touch* these vibrations, they would actually "convey a picture to your mind," of "the idea" that created them. (That is: the "idea *behind* the feelings," that are *producing* these vibrations).

... ("Whoa, man... I'm really getting some *vibes*!").

4. Now your spirit would absolutely *recognize* these vibrations as being "feelings." And the specific nature of these vibrations (meaning: their frequencies and wave shapes) would actually convey to the spirit, the particular "*character* of the feelings," that produced those vibrations.

It would tell her essentially, what those feelings "feel like."

And because your presence is actually well-versed in interpreting feelings in this manner, your person would then know precisely what those feelings are saying: "I'm conscious"; "I'm aware"; "I'm happy"; "I'm sad"; "I think I'll go over to Sheila's house"; or even: "E = M C-squared."

(What I'm saying here essentially is that, feelings

are sort of like a "computer language" for the mind. And really it is *the brain* actually, and not the spirit, that is able to understand this language.

(But the spirit you see is able "to utilize" the brain, to instantly *translate* these feelings, into thoughts and emotions [and into whatever else it is, that they are trying to convey]).

5. So these energy vibrations coming from the feelings of being conscious, and of being aware, are "pulsing energies," that are continuously pressing up against our living presence (and making direct physical contact with her).

One of them is an electrical awareness, *pushing* against her energy; and the other is a magnetic consciousness, *pulling* against it. (Pushing and pulling; pushing and pulling: on and on).

And as I say, these energy vibrations are really just carriers of "the states of mind" that produce them. So these vibrations are directly conveying to our spirit our "mortal mind's" two basic feelings: the feelings, of being conscious and of being aware.

6. (And as we will come to discover, not only do our consciousness and awareness produce being conscious and being aware, but [because they are indeed operational *parts* of our active intelligence] they are continuously, *independently* producing: ideas, and perceptions, and states of mind… just like our living presence is.

(And so of course, the vibrations of the luminous glows also convey, all of *these* various "feelings" to our spirit).

Chapter 20

1. … (And to pick up our narrative… from just after our spirit is first pulled into the luminous energies; there at the beginning of her Life as an organism)…

Now… as our spirit's light of conception begins to flood into the luminous energies, illuminating them, and causing them to emit these: "glows of expressed feeling"… the energy pulses from these two glows, as surging forces, begin pressing themselves, *into our spirit's* energy.

This causes her energy (in *its* turn) to essentially, begin "churning, and turning over." In other words her energy becomes active. It begins to work. (Basically, it starts to become operational, as a working part, of the organism's cognitive and emotional [and perceptual] systems).

And *how* conception energy works of course is: to conceive. And so our spirit is basically pushed (and pulled) into conceiving.

2. And *what* she begins to conceive of naturally, is these two pulsing feelings that are pressing up against her and "disturbing her energy." Because of course, these are the most immediately available things *for her* to conceive of.

(She is already as we know, conceiving of *herself* —sort of, subliminally… as an innate quality of her energy. [Meaning: her energy does not have to be "churning" for her to be able to conceive of herself]. But conceiving of something *other* than herself —that is, conceiving of something of *this* world— that's what we're really talking about here.

3. (… And really this is all pretty remarkable when you think about it.

(I mean, when we say that our spirit "*conceives* of the two pulsing feelings," what we're really saying is simply that, she "*becomes aware of*" these feelings. Or in other words really, *in effect*, she "*perceives* these feelings."

(But our spirit is just "a living energy." And as such, she does not have any kind of perception organs. So the only thing that our spirit is really *able* to be aware of —able that is, "to perceive"— *is her own energy*… and by consequence of course, "disturbances to that energy."

4. (So what I'm trying to point out is that, "*no special effort*" [or no "special tools," or anything like that] is required on our spirit's part, to be able to perceive the energies of our mind; and to perceive what they are doing.

(Because she *is able* "to perceive all of this," simply by: "being aware *of herself*"; and by perceiving how these energies, impact *HER* energy.

(But anyhow…).

Chapter 21

1 Okay. But let's take a look at the actual physics of this process.

Now, because these glows from the two luminous energies are actually pulsing *vibrations*… as they push up against our living presence then, these vibrations will be completely *transferred* to that presence energy.

And our spirit, who basically is just "sitting there" conceiving of her own energy, will unquestionably *notice* the disturbance, that these vibrations cause to her energy field.

So what she will do, is to focus her conception *upon* this disturbance. And as she does this, she is actually able *to conceive* of these "vibrations" (that is basically, she is able "to perceive them").

2. And because these energies are literally vibrating *feelings*, that are "conveying the applications of mind" that produced them… as our spirit then conceives of these vibrations, she is actually able to discern the cognitive, emotional, and perceptual operations that are *the source* of these feelings.

(All that I'm saying is that, as the luminous glows press into our spirit's energy, their vibrations, and the feelings and ideas being "carried" within those vibrations, all become "*absorbed into*" her energy.

(So our spirit is able "to perceive" these vibrations,

and the "sentient activity" they convey, as I say, by simply continuing to "perceive her own energy").

In other words, effectively, our spirit becomes aware of what the luminous energies: are "thinking," feeling, and/or perceiving.

And as we've mentioned... this is of tantamount importance to how our mind works. As we shall be seeing, this is what actually makes it possible for the three energies of our mind, *to be able* to work together: at "constructing a whole mind."

3. So because these energy pulses are feelings, and because our conception (our spirit) is *conceiving* of these feelings... it can then be said that essentially, our spirit actually begins: *"to feel"* the glows of the two luminous energies —as these energies go about being conscious and being aware.

Or we can really put this another way and say that, our spirit is basically beginning: *"to feel our mind*: being conscious, and being aware."

Or we can go even a step further and say that, by association, *our spirit herself* essentially, is beginning: *to become* conscious and aware. (Although of course, as l say, it is actually "the whole mind" —of which our spirit is just now becoming a part of— that is really becoming conscious and aware).

4. And I suppose we should stress at this point, that our living mind is not just something that *our spirit*, "becomes." What I mean is, as we shall be thoroughly exploring, the living mind is really, *a process of INTERACTION*... between our two mortal energies and our immortal presence.

And what I'm trying to point out here is that, if I haven't made it clear before, our luminous energies are really just as much a part of our active mind as our spirit is. Because consciousness and awareness is really something that *they* do. And our presence merely "conceives of them"… *AS* they go about being conscious and aware.

Because you see, our presence is really only an energy of "conception." And basically, as we've pointed out, the only thing that this energy can really do, is "to conceive" (in other words: to "imagine").

5. But as we've also suggested, our mind will of course, not *become* conscious and aware without our conception's input. So what in fact our conception actually does, "in order *to make* the mind conscious and aware"… is to sort of "tap-into" our consciousness and awareness; and as I say, simply: conceive of them.

And our two luminous energies *themselves* then make the mind conscious and aware, *AS* our spirit conceives of them.

Chapter 22

1 You might say in fact that our consciousness, awareness, and conception, are sort of like three soap bubbles sticking together... two larger bubbles, with a smaller bubble in the middle.

And where the smaller bubble, or our conception, touches the two larger bubbles —our consciousness and awareness— a sort of "hole" or something like that is opened up between conception and each of the other two energies.

And conception is then, able to actually "see into" these two mortal expressions of being alive.

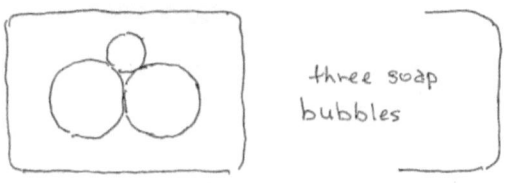

Illustration 10

2. And because *how* she will "see into" them, is by conceiving of them (... which means basically, she is not merely *perceiving* consciousness and awareness. She is actually getting *inside* of them; experiencing them from the inside out; as though these two feelings were actually her own person.

(In other words, she is fully "visualizing" what they are doing, as they go about creating being conscious and being aware.

(But… because how she "sees into them" as I say, is by actually "conceiving of them")… she is thus able to *fully experience* these two energies; as though indeed they were expressions of her own mind —that is, as though being conscious and being aware was actually what *she* was doing.

3. So though our conception does not herself actually *become* "conscious and aware," it really amounts to the same thing.

Chapter 23

1 And so our conception begins to conceive of her consciousness and awareness. Or... for our purposes here (meaning: in practical terms) you could really just say that, basically, she begins "to perceive" them.

But our conception (that is, our spirit) doesn't just say to herself: "... oh, there's a consciousness..."; and: "... oh: there's an awareness...."

Because the property of conception is really just a conception *of itself*. (As we've mentioned our spirit's real property is to conceive *of herself* being alive). So conception cannot really "keep itself out of the loop."

Therefore, anything our spirit brings her conception to bear upon, will always reflect to some degree or other, the fact that conception is a purely *subjective* quality: "... this is: *me* conceiving..."; "... this is what *I* am conceiving of..."; etc. etc.

2. So what our living presence (our spirit) actually does, and let me emphasize... quite erroneously... is to imagine, that indeed this consciousness and this awareness are actually *herself*. What I mean is that, she "sees" these two sentient properties, and immediately assumes: "... oh, that's *ME... I'M* conscious... and *I'm* aware...."

And really I suppose we should add that: "well what else *could* she think?" I mean she perceives this consciousness and awareness "inside of her own mind," as it were. And so naturally then, she just assumes that these two expressions of Life are really, *only herself*.

In other words, she assumes that this is what *she is doing*. S*he* is being conscious; and she, is being aware.

3. However, erroneously or not, once our conception begins to imagine that she herself is the author of this consciousness and awareness that she is perceiving… well, the very property: "*OF* imagining," acts as an applied force… that literally *seizes* upon —and holds onto— the energy of these two feelings.

What I'm saying is that, essentially, the instant that our spirit begins imagining that *she* is the one who's conscious and aware… the energy: of "the cognitive activity, of *imagination*"… actively reaches out, grabs hold of —and *binds*— all three of these living energies *together*, into a single "whole."

That is to say: into a whole living mind —that is conscious and aware, and able to conceive of itself.

4. And "the force of imagining" holds those energies together, *as* that living mind, as long as our spirit *continues to imagine* that she is conscious and aware.

(Which as we will come to see —imagining that she is conscious and aware— is something that our spirit is able to do even while we are asleep.

([And this is actually possible, because she is really imagining these things from the depths of our "subliminal mind"]).

5. Basically all I'm saying is that, believing that *she* is this consciousness and awareness that she perceives, *compels* our spirit "to hold onto" these two expressions of being alive. Because if our mind really believes something to actually "be itself", naturally then, it will automatically "clutch onto" that thing.

(Of course at this point of our development, our consciousness and awareness are expressed within us, in pretty much the same fashion that they are when we are asleep. [That is when we sleep, after we have been born].

(They are inert feelings way in "the back of our mind"; that are not really being expressed, well, as *intelligent* sentience, per se —but instead, as sort of a *dormant* sentience. Nevertheless, our spirit is able to perceive this "dormant" sentience… because her abilities of perception are very keen).

Part Five

Chapter 24

1. And so basically our mind begins to put itself together. Our consciousness and awareness come to Life and become an active (though for the time being essentially, an inert —well seers really say: a subconscious) force of expression.

And our conception "wakes up" into this world (that is: she wakes up into her subconscious mind), and begins perceiving that her mind is conscious and aware (though it is conscious and aware as I say, on a "sub" conscious level.

(Well we should probably pause and clarify this a little. Because though it may seem to us, that referring to "consciousness" as transpiring on a "*subconscious*" level of our mind, is actually a contradiction in terms [a misnomer], we will come to see that this is really not so. It's just an instance where our words fail us in fully defining a situation.

(Because our mind is definitely *still* conscious [and aware] on what seers would call: the subconscious level, of our mind's... "*attention*." [Although it is actually conscious and aware, from a much *deeper* "level of attention" than our waking, conscious mind. But we will be exploring this more fully]).

2. And thus, assuming that this is she herself who is going about being conscious and being aware, our conception embraces these two expressions of sentience; and "encompasses them within her idea" of who she is.

(You see the beauty of all of this? The world builds a body of mind energy for our spirit; and she moves *into* this mind energy and "claims it for herself." And by doing so our spirit turns this mind energy, *into*, a bona fide "mind"... manifestly, by becoming *a part* of that mind.

(Thus from that point on our spirit *has* a mind —and of course it's accompanying organism— as a means of actually participating, within the goings-on of the physical universe).

3. So all that we're really after here is to get a basic idea of how the mind is "assembled." And all that we really need to understand is that: our organism's mind springs to Life, when its three living energies begin interacting with each other.

And as I say, how these energies *begin* interacting is that: our spirit "sees her mind being conscious and aware," and she fully believes that she's merely seeing *herself*.

I mean, she believes that she in fact is the one who's being conscious and aware; when really all that she's doing is merely, "watching" her consciousness and awareness take place (independently really of anything that *she's* doing); while she goes about "imagining": "... oh; this is *me* doing all of this...."

4. And as our spirit imagines this —and indeed believes it to be so— this in fact is the single act that actually *starts* the mind's energies interacting with one another. Because this "belief" is what actually: "pulls the mind together", into behaving, like a single, whole mind.

Well that's not precisely so. I mean this belief is certainly what *initiates* the whole process. But it is actually, *the whole mind's*... "perception of itself"... that really starts the ball rolling. I mean, that's what really starts the mind's three sentient energies interacting with one another.

And how this comes about is that, as our spirit begins to perceive (what *she* will think of as) "her" feeling of (let's say for instance) being conscious... our consciousness, for its part, will actually *notice* our spirit doing this. (Because after all, they are both *living* energies, living within the same whole mind).

5. So what I'm saying is that, as our spirit begins "to feel the glow" of our consciousness energy —as it goes about being conscious— her reaction essentially, will be to "look" at that energy. That is, she will focus her "idea energy" *upon* this feeling.

And our consciousness will actually "see her" do that. He will perceive our spirit "looking at him." (In other words he will *feel* our conception, focusing her attention upon *him*).

And so as a consequence of seeing his spirit, two things will happen for consciousness. He will of course instantly become *aware* of his spirit. Because well, he is perceiving her. But consciousness will also become instantly *aware of himself*.

Because he sees that *he* is what his spirit is actually looking at. Thus he then, "notices himself" as it were. (What I mean essentially is that: he perceives himself, perceiving his spirit —*AS*... she is perceiving him).

6. And at the same time that all of this is happening, our spirit will also begin perceiving our feeling of awareness.

So naturally, because our awareness, conception, and consciousness are all parts of the same mind (and because consciousness has just begun perceiving our conception; and so then, is able to perceive what our conception is doing), our consciousness *will also* begin perceiving, our awareness.

And of course the same sort of process as happens to our consciousness will also happen with our awareness.

7. As our spirit begins to perceive our consciousness —and then also begins perceiving our awareness— our awareness (being part of the same whole mind that our spirit and consciousness are) will actually be able to "share" in our spirit's perception.

So he will also begin to perceive our consciousness. And he will begin to perceive our spirit; *as our spirit* begins to perceive our consciousness.

And of course, because our awareness notices that our spirit has actually begun to perceive *him* (our awareness) as well, he (our awareness) will thus also (through our spirit's perception of him), become aware of *himself.*

Whew!

Chapter 25

1 And as these three sentient energies then actually begin to perceive each other, it is *this* process that literally begins the continuing escalation: of the interaction, that *creates* the living mind.

Although in effect what has really happened, is that our spirit has "moved into" this machine of living mind energy, and brought it to Life; simply by conceiving of it.

I mean basically she has "turned the energy machine on," simply by *beginning to interact* with its energy. Which she does essentially, by *imbuing it*, with her conception of being alive... through the process: of going about "imagining" that *she* is the one who is conscious and aware.

And so, as the mortal mind energies are "imbued" in this manner with *"the conception of itself"* coming from our spirit, consciousness and awareness —who are indeed "living energies," but not actually "alive" before this all happens— are then "brought to Life"; because they are now able, basically, to *"imagine themselves"* as being alive.

2. So in a nutshell these are the proceedings that allow our spirit to "come down here" from her own dimension of existence, so that she can imagine —though what seers really say is: so that she can *"dream"*— that she is an organism, living the Life of an emotional being.

You see she simply *inhabits* the organism's energies of being conscious and being aware, in order to use these two sentient properties, to build a living mind for herself. And she then uses this living mind as her "instrument," for interacting with the physical universe, as an emotional being.

3. And again, the way in fact that *she manages* to inhabit these luminous energies, is through the simple expedient of imagining, that "she (indeed) *is* this consciousness" that she is perceiving, and that "*she* is this awareness."

(While of course, it's really "the organism's mind" that is conscious and aware [that is, as long as the spirit's light of conception is there, to keep the organism's mind energies "illuminated"; and *able to continue*, being conscious and being aware]).

Because this act of imagining —or let's say here: the act of "believing"— that *she herself* is this consciousness and this awareness, will produce expressions of force, that will literally bind her own living energy together, with the two *mortal* living energies.

Therefore together, they will then be able to begin expressing themselves, as a whole, living mind.

4. And just to be clear about it, let me emphasize that, our spirit's light of conception does not just *start* the luminous energies working. But up to this very moment, the reason that we are conscious and aware, is because the force of our conception's light, *continues* to shine upon these luminous energies.

And it continues to "turn those energies over" and "keep them churning." And until the day we die: this is what will keep us conscious and aware. (Even as we've suggested, during our sleep; where our mind *remains* conscious and aware —although from a state of near "stasis").

5. So unavoidably really, we're led to what may well strike you, as a fairly inconsequential observation. (However as we proceed with our narrative, it may tend to take on a bit more gravity for us).

And this observation is simply that: "while Life itself is undeniably a process of ongoing *sentience*; this ongoing Life is actually *put together* for us, as strictly, a moment to moment *energy process*."

In other words as living beings what we *really* are: is "energy machines." Because what keeps our mind actually going, from moment to moment... is the energy process: of the light of our spirit's "presence"... continuously "surging into" our luminous energies... and filling them, with our spirit's ongoing conception, of her own existence.

6. And as we've seen, being filled with our spirit's conception of herself, will *initiate* the energy process, which then impels our mind's two luminous energies: into becoming conscious, and into becoming aware (as *energy reactions*, you see, to our spirit's light).

And as we've also seen, as the two luminous energies in fact then *become* conscious and aware, they are each stirred into emitting a pressure —that is: a feeling— which will push back into the energy of presence; and subsequently, *compel* our presence, into believing that these feelings are her own being.

And believing this will cause her to "reach out" with

her conception, and tangibly "bind" these energies, *to* herself. And this simply means: that she will *hold onto* this consciousness and awareness.

(And basically, why she holds onto them is because: 1) she believes that she is actually "bringing these conditions about"; and: 2) she understandably, "wants her consciousness and awareness to continue").

7. And this is all one complete energy process —just a "loop"— that goes on and on, continuously, moment to moment, every instant of our lives. And through this process, not only do *we become* conscious and aware, but we also come to fully *perceive ourselves* as being so.

And so thereby (*through* this energy process) our ongoing Life as a living mind, is assembled for us... moment by moment. And we become conscious of ourselves, and aware of our environment.

Chapter 26

1 Nonetheless, once this whole energy process has gone ahead and put our mind together for us for the moment (by compelling the three individual energies of our mind to begin interacting with each other)... it is then unequivocally, the whole mind's *"realization of its own existence,"* which actually holds that Life together for us.

We "hold our Life together" you see, by imagining that indeed... *we are*... this living mind.

Well really though, that might be a little confusing: to say that *our whole mind* is what actually "holds our existence together" (by imagining itself to indeed *be* this whole mind). Because thus far we've only really mentioned that: "once *our spirit* perceives our consciousness and awareness," *she* imagines those two expressions of mind, to be *her*self.

(And so she then "holds onto" these two sentient properties, by thinking of them as a part of her whole being.)

2. Okay. But what we haven't really stressed yet is that, being sentient energies, once our consciousness and our awareness are "imbued" with our spirit's "conception of itself," they become fully capable of performing such feats of intelligence as: perceiving, and "believing."

Therefore, when *these luminous energies* perceive

our spirit —and her "surety of being" (and such things)— they instantly come to the conclusion (and we might once again call upon the phrase: "[and of course] quite erroneously"), that this in fact must be who *they are*.

What I'm saying is that, both of them *believes*, that he (individually) *is* this spirit, who conceives of her own existence. Well, they believe that this spirit is who they *also* are.

3. In other words they each believe, everything they perceive our spirit doing (because they don't really perceive her "person," as such... they only perceive what that person "is doing" [what she is thinking, or choosing, or focusing upon, etc. etc.]...

(But... they each believe everything they perceive our spirit doing)... is merely something that they are *themselves* (individually) doing.

Now you will notice we didn't really say, that how consciousness and awareness do this, is by: "*thinking of*" our spirit (that is: thinking of our spirit's *actions*) as being "their own person."

Because unlike our conception, our consciousness and awareness are not exactly *capable* of thinking. (*Their* energy can only "feel").

4. So seers say that what's really going on here is that the two luminous energies (pretty much just like our spirit), simply *include* our spirit's actions: into their "idea of themselves."

In other words as they perceive what our spirit is doing, they instantly just "accept this," as being something that *they* are doing.

And (while they're at it) they go ahead and do pretty much the same thing with each other. As each of them perceives what the other luminous energy is doing, each of them simply accepts this as being a part of himself. (Which is to say: as being who he *also* is.

5. (Do you see what we're really talking about here? Your mind is actually composed of three, *separate*, sentient energies; who *each* believe, that they are *YOU*...!

(And because they are all part "*of a whole mind*," they each believe: indeed, everything they see that mind doing... is merely something *they themselves*, have brought about....

(I mean, isn't "*your* mind" working like that? What I'm saying is, doesn't *all of your mind*, believe that it is you)?

6 Of course what consciousness and awareness are really doing you see, is exploiting our spirit's idea —her belief— that: "the whole mind, is who she really is"... to also look upon the whole mind, as *their* person.

You see, because the luminous energies are each "operational parts" of the same mind that our spirit is, they (or really, they, and our spirit as well) are able *to utilize*, anything that the other parts of the mind are doing.

So, the luminous energies will "borrow" our spirit's imagination (her concept: that *she* is this mind), and they will "borrow" each others' consciousness and awareness (to each be: conscious "of themselves," and aware: "of the whole mind"); so that they are then able to *look upon* the whole mind (and everything that the mind does) as being: who *they* are.

Chapter 27

1 And so our consciousness and awareness each "accept" the whole mind as being: who they are. Or in more practical terms you could say that essentially, they simply "believe this to be so." And as we've seen, this act of "believing" (as it does for our spirit), actually *effects* (or, brings about) their "holding onto" the mind.

And as all three of the mind's energies are doing this very thing (they are holding onto the mind, *through*, the process: of "believing it to be themselves") this is then what literally "binds the whole mind together, into a whole."

2. And really all I'm trying to say here is that, not only does *our spirit* imagine herself to be alive, and to in fact, herself, be our whole mind, but our two luminous energies (once our spirit begins to accept *them* as a part of her mind) are able "to borrow" our spirit's imagination, so that they can *also* imagine, that *they* are alive.

And so that they can each also imagine, that they themselves (individually) are actually: the whole mind that *they* perceive.

… Well it's not exactly that the luminous energies are *themselves* able, to *literally*: "imagine that they are alive"; and that they are our person's whole mind. Because imagining is a property of our conception's energy.

Instead, being a *functioning part* of our whole mind, these energies, essentially (as we will shortly see), are able to: *precipitate* the whole mind, into imagining these things *for them*.

But it really amounts to the same thing.

3. And this might be a good place to mention that this whole process: of the three living energies being able to perceive each other; and then believing these other energies to actually be themselves... really creates, well, sort of a bizarre situation.

What it does, is to help "reverse everybody's roles." And this is actually a very important part of how the mind functions.

You see, even though our conception is really our mind's imagining energy, and our luminous body is our mind's feeling energies, these two types of energy essentially end up, "commandeering" each others' energy properties; and pretty much, neglecting their own.

Let's look at how this works.

4. Now our conception is the one who really does "the imagining," or let's just say: "the thinking" for the mind. Because that's simply what her energy does.

But because our consciousness and awareness are each assuming that our "thinking processes" are just another part of *them*selves —and because our conception ("our real thinker") is essentially "busy elsewhere" (she is busy believing that our "*feeling* processes," are what *she is doing*)— and of course naturally, because these three sentient energies are all, merely *parts* of the same whole mind... well... our luminous energies are then easily able, to pretty much *tell* our conception, *what to think*.

5. Well actually though, that's not totally accurate. More precisely, what the luminous energies do is that: they tell the mind, what *they*... "*want the mind*... to think."

Or really, even better yet: because each of the luminous energies believes that *he* is our thinking processes, neither of them would then actually "go to the trouble" of literally, "telling the mind" what they want it to think. Because they're certain that the mind will *already* think, what *they* are wanting it to.

So all that they really do, is to simply: "*evoke the feeling* within themselves," that *proclaims*: "what the mind '*should be*' thinking." (That is, essentially, they "evoke the feelings" that will then actually, *trigger* the desired thoughts, from "our mind's conception").

And because our conception believes that these two luminous feelings are merely herself, well, she really has no problem with all of this. She simply assumes that indeed, this is only what *she* wants to be thinking. So she just goes ahead and "thinks like that."

6. And it's really the same sort of thing with our mind's "feelings." Our consciousness and awareness of course, are the ones who actually "*do* the feeling" for the mind. Because that's what *their* energy does.

But because these luminous energies are also "busy elsewhere" —they are busy telling our conception "*what to think*"— well, our conception is easily able to "tell" the luminous energies: *what to feel*.

Or like I say how such a thing works is that, she basically "indicates to the mind", what "*she wants*" the mind to feel. (And really how she does this actually, is by simply, "*expecting* the mind," to feel this way. [We will be exploring this more thoroughly]).

7. And likewise, the luminous energies also have no trouble with these state of affairs. Because, each of them believes, that our mind's conception is actually just "another piece" of what *they are*.

So, whenever our conception manages to convey what she wants "to feel"… the luminous energies are convinced that this is merely what *they* want to feel. So they essentially, just go ahead and produce that feeling.

And this is all no big deal really. Seers say that Life has been devised to work like this. (Which is to say, that Life has "designed Itself" to work in this fashion). I mean, this is simply the way that the mind has *evolved itself* into functioning.

Chapter 28

1 But why is this so? And more than that, how does this all come about really? What I mean is, what actually *causes* our feeling energies to believe that *they* are the mind's thinking energies; and, what causes our spirit to believe, that *she* is our mind's "emotional energies"?

Well the reason all of this happens, is because that's pretty much the only way that the mind *can* really work.

You see, the mind's three sentient energies end up basically: "watching each other... *all the time*." What I'm saying is that, our spirit (for instance) "watches our feeling energies"... *continuously*.

But she is actually *compelled* into doing this. What I mean is that, she really has no choice, *but*, to watch these energies all of the time.

2. Because once she begins conceiving of the sentient properties that these energies produce (the properties of being conscious, and of being aware), she simply *must* watch those energies all of the time, in order to "hold onto them." What I'm saying is that, our spirit must "hold onto" the luminous energies, if she wants to be able *to continue* conceiving of their properties; that is, if she wants to continue "*being* conscious and aware."

Because, as the luminous energies are not actually

her own energy, if she didn't continuously "hold onto them" —by "watching them" all the time… or as I say: by *conceiving* of them all of the time— she wouldn't "be able to find" her consciousness and awareness anymore.

And of course the whole mind then, would simply cease being.

3. And so, "as a consequence" really, of *continuously conceiving of* her consciousness and awareness… she actually *comes to believe* that "this feeling": *is who she really is*. And so in effect, she basically "*becomes* this feeling"… essentially, by "assuming its operation."

What I'm saying is that, our spirit pretty much "abandons" *her own* energy properties, so that she can more easily believe, that she is our mind's emotional energies. (Well… she essentially abandons: *selecting* what the mind "will think"; in order to focus upon: what the mind "will feel").

And as we've mentioned, that's really what our spirit has actually come here to do: "*to dream* that she is an emotional being."

4. And its pretty much the same sort of thing for our consciousness and awareness. They must continuously "hold onto" our conception, if they want her, or really we should say: if they want *the whole mind*, to continue "to imagine" *for them*… that they are alive.

So they will simply tend to focus their attention, that is their *perception*, upon *her* (or more to the point really, upon her energy property of "imagining"). And basically, they will *continuously* keep their perception focused upon our spirit and her energy properties.

And so, as a consequence of perceiving our spirit's

energy properties continously, fundamentally they will (as I say) *commandeer* her energies; and for the most part really, disregard their own.

So what I'm saying is that, essentially, *they* become our mind's "thinkers," while our conception, basically becomes, our mind's "emotional intelligence."

And as with our spirit, this happens really *as a consequence*, of keeping their perception continuously focused upon our mind's conception.

5. But like I say, none of these three energies has any problem with all of this. I mean, they certainly don't *miss* their own energies... because they are each still living there, *within* their own energy.

And they are in fact each, still "operating" their own energy; because of course, no one else *can*. And they don't notice someone else is "commanding, *how* they operate their energy."

Because they all believe, these "commands" coming from the mind's "other two energies," are merely *their own mind*, doing its job.

6. And as I say, this is all helping to fulfill the universe's purpose, of allowing our spirit "to dream" that she is an emotional being, living in a physical reality. She in effect "dreams," that she is our mortal feeling; while our two luminous energies in effect "dream," that they are our mind's imagining energy.

(And actually... by "commandeering," and *using* each other's energies in this fashion, *this* more than anything else really, is what *mostly* enables, these energies to "hold onto each other", for the purposes of creating a whole mind).

Chapter 29

1 And so, though "*being* alive" actually puts itself together, entirely, as an act *of energy*... "Life Itself" then, will literally *sustain* It's ongoing existence: through an *act of mind*... that is, through an act of "imagination."

This is to say that, manifestly, we are alive as a living mind, because we *tell* ourselves that we are alive —that is, *because we imagine* that we are alive. Or better yet, we are alive because: we *continuously* imagine, that we are in fact, *being* alive.

And this indeed, is what allows us to hold onto the Life process... that the universe of "energy, *machine processes*" so generously puts together for us, moment by moment.

(So if you were an acute observer, you might even see these two processes taking place in your own mind. The process of your living energies: putting your Life together; and then the process of your living mind: keeping that Life going).

2. And we might mention that, by actually conceiving of our mind's consciousness and awareness as being her own expressions of mind... not only is our spirit grabbing onto these energies, and clutching them to herself (thereby helping *to bind* the mind's three living energies together); but essentially, she is also using these energies, to pull herself *fully into* the physical

realm.

Because up until the moment that our spirit actually begins to feel the pressures, of the "glows" that are coming from her mind's consciousness and awareness, pushing up against her as feelings; she isn't really quite "inside" of the luminous body just yet.

I mean she hasn't fully *let go* of her own dimension; but is sort of "hanging there within the dimensional rift" —half-in, and half-out.

3. But once she actually begins imagining that this consciousness and this awareness that she perceives, are really (as she believes) *her own* manifestations of being; she has at that point let us say: successfully used these energies, to "grab onto, and pull herself" fully into the luminous body, you see.

And thus she then begins fully "dwelling within the luminous body." And her Life as an emotional being, in the physical universe, can be said to have rightly begun.

4. Of course, for some time forward (as the organism is growing within the womb) our spirit will be almost entirely, "fast asleep and dreaming." But at a very deep level of her conception she already fully realizes, that she has indeed undergone an amazing transformation; and has become an emotional being who "feels."

You see, she perceives that she has progressed from being just a simple "presence" —who can do nothing more really than to simply conceive of herself— into being an entire living mind; that is both conscious of itself, and aware of its environment.

Admittedly this would be a very limited awareness,

and consciousness, within the womb. But nevertheless "Life" has begun.

5. So all in all, it has come to pass you might say, that our immortal presence has indeed "come to this world of emotion," and conjoined with the mortal energies of our physical body's "mind," in order to enhance the scope of her existence. That is: in order to gain a broader range of ongoing experience.

Or if you want to look at all of this from the viewpoint of energy: the physical universe has once again "snagged itself," a piece of the great Spirit of Life's immortal essence. (Because from the viewpoint of energy, that's all that an individual spirit really is: just "a piece" of the dimension of living presence).

6. So the universe will now compel this spirit *to remain* upon this level of existence. And it will also compel her, to actually *address herself* to this physical environment; so that *through* that process, Life can "be expressed" —which of course is Life's purpose: to be expressed.

(Life is being expressed you see, as an individual living being, struggling with its environment).

And by impelling "the expression of Life" (through the process of compelling our spirit into an *interaction* with the physical environment), the universe can thereby fulfill *ITS* purpose: of being *a habitat* for Life; a place within which Life can dwell, and flourish.

Afterword
the little boy and the fish

1 Once there was a young man who wished to become a storyteller. Now storytellers in those days were well-respected people. There was really no place that they couldn't go, without being able to draw a large and appreciative crowd around themselves; a crowd who would be more than willing to cough up a few small coins to reward an artful recitation, of a favorite popular-tale.

So the young man searched the country far and wide to find a teacher that he could apprentice himself to, for however long it took, in order to learn the art of storytelling. And so, after a long and arduous quest, the young man finally located a highly renowned teacher; who agreed to teach the young man his art.

For five long years the young man stayed at the teacher's house. To repay his teacher for the efforts of instructing him, the young man became practically the teacher's servant. All day long he would scrub and clean to his teacher's satisfaction; he would carry water, and carry wood; he would sweep the inside of the house, and sweep around the outside; he would work in the garden; do laundry; and rake leaves.

Once or twice a day however, the teacher would have the young man take a break from his chores, and would have him recite the story: of *the little boy and the fish*; which was a very old, and very popular folktale that his teacher had taught him.

Now of course, the young man didn't really mind performing all of these daily chores for his teacher. Because this was how the traditional relationship between a teacher and a student took place in those days; and was something which the young man had fully expected anyway.

However, what did actually trouble the young man though, was that for all of these years, day in and day out, the only story that the teacher would have the young man to recite, was the story of: *the little boy and the fish.*

And the young man's patience was running pretty thin. "Doesn't the fellow *know* any more stories?" the young man would often ask himself. Because, after all of this time, he had fully expected you see, to have an entire repertoire of stories under his belt.

2. But the teacher had taught him only the one story; and if you were inclined to judge from the teacher's appraisals of the young man's recitations, the young man had not once, actually told the story to his teacher's satisfaction.

Understandably, feeling somewhat daunted by all of this, it took every effort on the young man's part to resist the urge of accusing his teacher of just stringing him along; getting him to work as a servant, without even teaching him any stories. (Or as I say, without teaching him any more than just this one, single story).

But just when the young man would reach the point where he could no longer stand the tension, and was ready to accuse the teacher to his face of taking advantage of their agreement, the teacher would sit the young man down, and expound upon his inadequacies as a storyteller.

"You have no real appreciation for the ironies and the subtleties of the story," was the kind of things that the teacher would comment upon. "Do you suppose that your *listeners* then, will supply these things themselves? Or don't you think that it is really *your* responsibility to bring these things out?

"You fumble with the thread of the story: you rush here, when you should go slow; and you hesitate there, when you should push on.

"You don't describe your characters as though it were actually *important*, that your listeners should have a complete understanding of the turmoil within their minds —being confronted with the situations that they are encountering.

"You describe the scenery, as though you were ordering fish at the market; as if you really didn't care that it was a crucial part of your recitation, for your listeners to actually '*see*' the land through which your characters are passing... as if they were actually standing there themselves.

"How can I possibly give you other stories to learn, as you've so often asked me to do; when, after all of these years of trying, you haven't even mastered this one?"

3. Of course the teacher's comments were always dead on the mark. The young man realized that fully well. But nonetheless, the question of his teacher's sincerity, and of his earnestness in his teaching methods notwithstanding, the young man finally came to the conclusion that his teacher was really just some kind of nut; and had no talent at all for teaching storytelling.

The young man decided that he had made a mistake in becoming the teacher's apprentice; and that his teacher would never teach him more than the one, same story.

And so, after a sleepless night of agonizing, the young man got up early in the morning, and ran away from his teacher's house; taking the road that led out of that country.

All day long he traveled. He walked over hills, and he walked through valleys. He walked through patches of forest, and he walked through large open fields.

As dusk was beginning to fall he came upon a cozy looking little inn, tucked away some little distance from the road. He had no money but he ventured inside anyway, hoping to perhaps reap a little charity from its inhabitants.

4. As the young man walked through the door, he saw right away that it was indeed a cozy little place. The patrons were sitting comfortably and noisily around the inn's tables; laughing, talking, eating and drinking, and gesticulating with their arms, to drive a point or two home.

After pausing just inside of the doorway... for a somber, yet hopeful glance... the young man sought the innkeeper out, and humbly accosted him about the possibility of securing some food and lodging.

"Well…" the innkeeper answered the young man's inquiries, "… we certainly have victuals enough to spare; and we could no doubt put you up somewhere. But we are not in the custom really, of providing these services without some type of recompense.

"As you have no money, is there not something that you could do to repay us for these kindnesses? You are not perhaps a musician by any chance, are you?"

Well, the young man of course had to admit to the innkeeper that, no... he was *not* a musician, by any means; but that rather, instead... (and here he paused for a moment, considering; before he threw caution to the wind and plunged ahead)... that he did know one story that he could tell.

He then confessed that indeed, he had been an apprentice these last several years, of a renowned storyteller... but that he had finally run away; because for some reason or other, his teacher it seemed, had been unwilling to impart his art to the young man.

But, perhaps he could tell the one story that the teacher had taught him; and the innkeeper and his patrons could then judge, whether it had been worthy of any consideration, that they might then feel inclined of parting with.

5. So... the innkeeper gave the young man an understanding nod, and attracting the attention of his patrons, explained the situation to them. Some of them looked a little doubtful, but everyone loves a good story; and, evidently deciding that they didn't really have much to lose, they gestured for the young man to proceed.

When the young man announced that the story he was going to tell was that of: *the little boy and the fish*, he drew more than one appreciative glance; and his listeners it seemed, sat back a little more comfortably, as if the experience would perhaps not be quite so bad as they had supposed that it might.

The young man very quickly connected with his audience. It was almost magical. Indeed, it amazed the young man how impeccably, his timing and cadence seemed to flow, so effortlessly, out of him. And his dramatic pauses didn't seem a bit contrived; but seemed to be the most natural things in the world. Five minutes into the story, and every man, woman, and child, was hanging upon every word that he spoke; as if their very lives depended upon it.

The story took on a Life of its own. The room, and the inn, disappeared. The people were not sitting there, upon benches, and in chairs... they were walking with the little boy down by the river; searching for the very spot that his grandfather had told him about —where the river willows grew just to the edge of the water... and where the bank was only just high enough, where a little boy such as himself, could reach down while lying on his belly, and touch the water.

It was not as if the people had *to imagine* the little scene at the river. They could actually *smell* the willow trees; and feel the breeze, as it wafted up the bank. They could *see* the eyes of the little fish, as it swam to the surface to look at the boy.

"... I am so hungry," it said. "... the big fish get all of the food around here; and none is left for me. Yet were I to eat your worm, you would jerk the hook into my belly, and pull me out of the river for your own dinner. Can't you help me out, please? Someday, you yourself might be in need, like I am today."

Tears were in the eyes of every one of his listeners, and running down their cheeks. People unashamedly honked into their handkerchiefs —even the big, burly blacksmith; who was practically bawling like a baby at this point in the story.

6. When the young man reached the dénouement of his story, where the fish —who had since grown into a large, healthy specimen— was able to save the little boy (who had also grown, but was still just a boy) from drowning in the swollen river... as payment for his kindness years before: of feeding his only worm to the little fish —who had been virtually on the point of dying from starvation (and which act had resulted of course, in the little boy's having no opportunity for catching his own dinner that day... and so he had gone hungry that evening).

Well, when the fish saved the boy from drowning in the swollen river, and then revealed to the boy that he was the same little fish whose Life the boy had saved years before... the dam burst!

The people were actually blubbering and sobbing. They were hugging each other, and crying out loud. The young man couldn't believe his eyes. He had certainly not expected anything like this from his listeners. They ran up to the young man, and were literally falling all over each other, in their efforts to embrace him and kiss him on the cheek; while stuffing coins in his pocket. They were wringing his arm so heartily, that he was actually afraid they would injure it.

"Oh, we forgive you; we forgive you, alright..." they were all saying, confusing the young man at first as to their meaning; "... but why did you have to represent yourself as merely an amateur? It's quite evident that you are a consummate *master* in the art of storytelling. Never… never have we heard a story come to Life, such as you have told it; we forgive you for deceiving us. We will remember this night for many years to come. Now, please, come and dine with us."

And the people feasted the young man, and put him up in the best room that night, that the inn had to offer.

7. The next morning, after a hearty breakfast, and an emotional leave-taking, the young man was once again upon his way. A long night of soul-searching had answered many questions for him.

He now perceived that his teacher was a true master instructor in the art of storytelling. He understood that his teacher had taught him, not stories, but actually the art itself, of *telling* a story.

He had been compelled by his teacher to tell the same story so many times, that the story itself had actually ceased to exist for him. When he finally came to tell the story *to an audience* for the first time, he realized that his attention, almost unbeknownst to himself, was not really on the story itself; but actually, upon his listeners. It was they, who, through his "perception of their emotions," had managed to commune to the young man how to proceed with the story.

He had found himself shrewdly observing them for some reaction, like he had done so many times before with his teacher: trying to establish some kind of emotional connection with them, so that he would thus be more able to appraise what would please them, and what would not.

But they were a much "easier room" than his teacher

had been —who had always merely sat with a detached air, and with an easy, yet strict attention; simply *watching him* as he told his story. The audience in the inn had *wanted* to be entertained; and the young man had, to his great delight, found himself well able to accommodate them… to discern, and serve their every emotional craving.

8. The young man was now fully able to perceive, that the true art his teacher had taught him, was not even storytelling really... but actually, observation.

And "this realization" had, to his great surprise, literally "affected him" somehow. Something inside of him had actually *changed*, when he reached this understanding. And he could not really explain "why" that had happened; but nonetheless, it was really quite evident.

Because somehow, something in him that had been "closed," was now "opened"… if you can see what I mean. He was now an "awakened man"… as he saw it. Everything looked differently to him somehow. Perhaps, he mused, that was because he was now "really looking at things."

But he was wise enough to perceive this change in himself, not really as the crowning touch to his years of study; but instead, as his education's true beginning.

He smiled to himself, as he watched a hawk in the distance, gliding upon the winds. He had had not the slightest bit of hesitation as he left the inn that morning and walked to the road. Without even thinking, he had turned back to the direction from which he had come… back towards his teacher's house.

...And In Closing...

You know, in the end, being alive is really just "a frame of mind"... just a way "of looking at things."

I mean it's perfectly normal to complain; or to bemoan your fate. Because Life is hard. When so many living beings are thrown together, struggling for the same resources, it really couldn't be any other way.

But the way that *you perceive this Life* is really all up to you. I mean, it's *your job* to create a frame of mind that brings you the peace and the joy that we all crave; and that will do justice and honor, to this marvelous gift that was bestowed upon us...

(... inadvertently you might even say... one cloudy day).

So.

... And if you would, let us close with a seer's prayer of invocation.

O, Creator of the cosmos...
O, Spirit of this world...
We come to you with open hearts...
Deal unto us, with mercy...

www.ingramcontent.com/pod-product-compliance
Lightning Source LLC
LaVergne TN
LVHW041847070526
838199LV00045BA/1488